An incredible, true story of an unstoppable girl, determined to climb out of each pit and over every obstacle to succeed. Proof that a "go-getter" can create a fulfilling, satisfactory, and accomplished life. Phyllis, in the short time I've known her, has truly amazed me and inspired me to "get up and go for it" in my life and reach for my dreams! She's a very admired and loved friend who gives life to everyone she meets.

—Linda M. Metzger-Larson

Phyllis, as I know her today, is a healthy, happy, and successful businesswoman. To know her today you would not know that she only went through part of the ninth grade. You could say she got her education from the streets—the old-fashioned way, from just doing it. She had a difficult childhood and had to grow up fast. She is a perfect example of making the most of things and turning her life around. This book is a must-read. It is very inspiring to the American dream.

—Mary Adam

This fast-moving, real-life story of "behind the scenes" at the carnival is Phyllis Horne's riveting autobiography. She takes you from a dysfunctional and abusive childhood and life on her own from age fourteen, to her current roles of successful property owner, manager, grandmother, and, now, author. Phyllis has had more trials and successes in her life than most of us could survive in five lifetimes! Through tenacity, perseverance, and her "angels," Phyllis's adventures will keep you moving quickly through her book—almost asking for more!

I have also owned my own successful business and am not afraid to take on new challenges. God, too, has directed my life in a positive way! I have only known Phyllis for about two years, and she is one of my favorite people. I like her positive "can-do" attitude!

I highly recommend this inspiring, true-life story to anyone wanting inspiration to "keep on keepin' on"—no matter your educational background, financial status, or current situation!

—Cherry Jones
Former business owner, marketing instructor,
and Christian Women's Connection speaker and chairman

I remember going to the carnival when I was young—most of us do. I loved the games, cotton candy, rides, music, and the atmosphere of fun. But my mom always cautioned me about the carnies—like they were an unsavory group. In her book *The Carnival Girl*, Phyllis Horne teaches of the carnies' side of life, love, and family. She writes with a plea for others to see inside a carny's "little town on wheels" and learn about her journey out of difficult circumstances. A fascinating read!

—**Cindy Valenti-Scinto**
Speaker and author, *A Heart Like Mine* Trilogy

The Carnival Girl takes a behind-the-scenes look at one of America's favorite summer adventures. Most of us can remember screaming our lungs out on the carnival rides or stuffing our faces with cotton candy and other treats. And of course we always had to exercise our skills at the game booths in the hopes of just one big stuffed animal for our collections. But we never knew the people who actually lived with the carnival. Phyllis takes the reader on a journey to understanding what life was like for the real people of the carnival world. It's a journey of brokenness, a journey of joy, and a journey of love that you will never forget.

—**D. Faye Higbee**
Author

This book is the story of Phyllis growing up in the carnival. It opens our eyes to an extraordinary lifestyle of how she left the carnival with her young child, proved that with guts and determination one can make a complete turnaround, changed her profession, started her own business, bought a home, and retired with a pension. She is well respected in her neighborhood and church. This is her first novel. It is a zestfully informative and entertaining read. It is a book like no other.

—**Joan S. Hust, D.Litt.**

An exciting, true story by Phyllis Horne living the carny life. A story full of adventure, and a true love story. She writes about many hardships but also many fun adventures in her book. A must-read. You will truly enjoy this book.

—Sherelyn Holecek

This book is a must-read. I wanted to write it myself, but it is her story and true. I have known Phyllis for more than thirty years, and she has had the most interesting life and done more than anyone I have ever known. I am a retired real estate broker with forty years' experience, and I have met many people and seen many things, but she is the most interesting. We worked together for more than ten years, and it was an experience—once I suggested she should do something, she did it. She built her own home and subdivided some land, all with no prior experience. What a trip! You should enjoy this book.

—Alberta Spence

The unlikely and compelling story of a teenage runaway from a dysfunctional family into a vagabond life. Dramatic insight into the subculture life of a "carny." Definitely a primer on survival in a world most of us will never see, complete with a happy ending.

—Travis Jones
Col. (Ret.), USAF

THE
CARNIVAL
GIRL

To Shane!

THE CARNIVAL GIRL

Its great to know You!

One Woman's Journey Through the Carnival Life

Phyllis Horne

Phyllis Horne

I hope you enjoy this book!

WinePressPublishing
Great Books, Defined.

© 2011 by Phyllis Horne. All rights reserved.

WinePress Publishing (PO Box 428, Enumclaw, WA 98022) functions only as book publisher. As such, the ultimate design, content, editorial accuracy, and views expressed or implied in this work are those of the author.

No part of this publication may be reproduced, stored in a retrieval system or transmitted in any way by any means—electronic, mechanical, photocopy, recording, or otherwise—without the prior permission of the copyright holder, except as provided by USA copyright law.

Unless otherwise noted, all Scriptures are taken from the *Holy Bible, New International Version®, NIV®*. Copyright © 1973, 1978, 1984 by Biblica, Inc.™ Used by permission of Zondervan. All rights reserved worldwide. www.zondervan.com

ISBN 13: 978-1-4141-1960-1
ISBN 10: 1-4141-1960-7
Library of Congress Catalog Card Number: 2010938422

This book is dedicated to
My loving son, Bradley Horne

Who lived much of my trying life with me,
Who now has reaped some of the same rewards,
Who also has been my very best gift from God.

One of my biggest dreams has been to open a home for homeless teens. Street living is a very lonesome and hard life. It's a hard way to get started in life—you cannot know unless you've been there. I want to give them hope for their dreams. I want to show them that there is a higher power and that they can invite that higher power to be their partner in life. That higher power is always there, even if they're not aware of it. This book is as close as I'm going to get to that dream.

I truly wanted to get the word out to have faith and never to give up on your dreams. Your dreams will change as you go along in life, and some never go away completely. My dreams changed when I had a child and became responsible for another human being's life—everything changed as I once knew it. I truly hope I have touched people's lives—inspired them to fulfill their dreams and be in charge of their own destinies.

Try saying hello to your higher power and see how you can empower your life. Ask your higher power to be your partner, and watch everything change in your life. Just remember, you are the director of your own play in life, so make it the best you can be.

Blessings,
Phyllis

Contents

Acknowledgments xv

Introduction xvii

Prologue xxi

What Is a Carnival? xxvii

   1. Growing Up Fast 1
   2. Having Fun at the Carnival 13
   3. Back to My Childhood 17
   4. Back to Coeur d'Alene, Idaho, at Seventy Years Young 21
   5. Running Away to a New Life 25
   6. Getting Out of Jail 33
   7. I Booked a Train Ride to St. Louis, Missouri 37
   8. The Pike and Getting Married 41
   9. Indian Country 43
  10. Leaving the Reservation 51
  11. Bought Two Concessions on The Pike
      at Eighteen Years Old 57
  12. A New Life with Artie 63

13. Traveling with the Carnies 67
14. Bought My First Home 73
15. Back on the Road. 75
16. Back to Coeur d'Alene, Idaho 83
17. Entering the World of Real Estate. 87
18. Impressions of the Carnival 91
19. Real Estate in Rio Linda, California 101
20. Brad and Firewood 111
21. Carnival in the '60s. 115
22. Snowstorm Breaks all Records
    Since 1890 and Thanksgiving 125
23. Carnival Memories 129
24. Back to Idaho and Sunday Get-Togethers. 133
25. Thinking About the Carnival and Watching the Snow. . . 137
26. Torrance, California, to Cave Junction, Oregon,
    and the Yellow Submarine 145
27. Changing My Life 153
28. Philippines 161
29. My Motivation Started When I Was a Child. 165
30. Back to My Real Estate Story in Sacramento. 167
31. When We First Arrived in Oregon 169
32. Brazil 173
33. Saving the Owl, Starving the People 183
34. Moving to Idaho, Our Last Frontier 193

Acknowledgments

A SPECIAL THANKS to all the people that helped me along the way, with the sharing of their time, love, and patience with writing this book. To my great teachers of life: Lewis Bostwick, Michael and Raphaelle Tamure, who are also my dear friends. Lewis Bostwick has passed to the other side, but I will never forget him or be able to thank him enough.

To my good lifetime friend, Alberta Spence, who has always encouraged me to write a book and tell my story. To Sherelyn Holecek, who is my new friend that introduced me to a writer's class, taught by teacher Joan Hust. To my dear friend and teacher Joan Hust, who has inspired and helped me from the beginning to the end of writing this book. This book would not be if it wasn't for Joan Hust.

To all my editors and helpers: Faye Higbee, Travis and Cherry Jones, Donna Morey, and others at the Idaho Writers League. To Cindy Scinto, who was one of my last editors and had put a lot of time into editing and helping me with this book.

To God and his angels who have always been my partners in life—it just took me a long time to be aware of that. They have always protected me all through my life. Lots of love and thanks from the bottom of my heart to all my angels from above and right here on earth.

Introduction

THIS BOOK IS for young girls, middle-aged women, and golden girls; and for all men and women who want to fulfill their dreams. I had dyslexia and never learned how to spell, wasn't good at math, didn't learn much while I was in school, and didn't finish ninth grade. I was too busy having emotional problems. I was learning how to survive.

In 1956 at fourteen years old, I ran away and joined the carnival. This is my story of an adventurous ride and how I learned to think outside the box. It is the story of my dance with life. When you read of my time with the carnies, I am referring to the family of people who set up, operate, work hard at and travel with local carnivals. The days are long, and the lifestyle is like a gypsy. I want to show you the other side of carnies—the close ties and relationships that make traveling with a carnival fun and exciting. It's like having your own little town on wheels.

When I was a teenager I lived under a bridge before traveling with the carnies. It was an exciting and adventurous life. I'm finally telling this story with the hope it will inspire other runaways and young people that there is hope for their lives. You can do anything you set your mind to do, but you must have faith and ultimately trust God has a plan for you. I'm living proof it is possible. Have faith like the little children. Love God and he will work with you right by your side. He will be your partner.

> Unless you change and become like children you will never enter the kingdom of heaven.
> —Matt. 18:3

When you're young, you have the whole world at your feet for the taking. Have faith you can make something of yourself. If you make a mistake, get up and start over again until you reach your vision.

I'll never forget how scared I was, always running and always afraid the police would find me and take me back to juvenile hall. I feared going back to Torrance, California, where my mom lived in a twenty-foot trailer with her boyfriend—at least, her boyfriend at the time.

When I was fourteen years old, I ran away to Long Beach, California, and started working at an amusement park called The Pike. The Pike was a street a mile long that was completely lined with amusements, food vendors, and rides. It was operated by the famous Charles I. D. Looff, who is known for building the first carousel at Coney Island, New York, in 1875. The Pike opened in 1902 and had a roller coaster that extended out over the ocean.

I was fortunate to get that job. I had looked for work at every place in town and nobody would hire me. They all laughed at me and said I was too young. I looked like I was twelve years old, and they all assumed I was a runaway. Their advice was to "go home and come back in a few years."

The carnies on The Pike gave me that first job, and I worked there for ten years. After four years, I bought two concession stands and operated them for the next six years on The Pike. This all occurred before I went on the road with the traveling carnival.

The Pike was located on a beach with the finest pure-white sand. It set off all the beauty needed for a perfect picture. I should have taken pictures. I never can replace that time or visit that beautiful beach again. But I can always remember.

I don't talk much about my days when I lived and worked on The Pike. Nor do I talk about my eleven years traveling with the carnies throughout Arizona, Nevada, and California. I was afraid most people would not like or trust me anymore if I let too much of my past be known. It's a different life and most people wouldn't understand, I thought. But we were like everybody else except we had our little town on wheels.

The same families worked together each year at the carnivals. We helped each other out when needed. We were one big family. We respected each other and enjoyed putting on the show together. We took a lot of pride in doing the show right and making sure people had a lot of adventure and fun.

At times, unknown businessmen would drive up to the back of the show in their black limos with tinted windows. They funded the carnival, but we never got to see who they were. Rumor had it that without them we wouldn't have been having a show at all. To this day I don't know who those investors were, but God bless them. They fed a lot of people and kept us working.

It's interesting how some things in life seem like an illusion. Five different people can see and hear the same thing and then all come out with a different story. Life in the carnival is partially an illusion. It's different things to different people. Whatever the perception people have is what we'd try to fulfill.

I don't think there is anything wrong with performing for people to have fun. The carnival gives people a break from life. We all want to escape from the real world, feel free, and have fun like we did when we were little children.

You might think my stories are outdated, and maybe some are. But I bet if you looked real hard, they all relate to our business world today. Behind closed doors, people don't really change; they just get a little smarter. I believe human nature is human nature, and hopefully we include integrity, honesty, and love for all as we go along our path. I hope our children learn to appreciate our stories and life lessons.

I want this story to touch your heart and maybe spur your memories so you can write your stories for your children and their children to read and enjoy.

The Carnival Girl

A co-worker and I working in a shooting gallery on The Pike, in Long Beach California, at the age of 14 years old in 1956.

Prologue

"HEY, RUBE! LET'S rumble!"

When I first saw the Ferris wheel blink its lights on and off and the carnies stop their rides and jump across the counters, I knew it was time to move fast. They ripped off their aprons and threw them in the corners and ran like heck. I knew this routine by heart. Soon everybody was running by me and screaming, "Hey, Rube!"

I ripped off my apron and threw it in the corner of the joint. We had a new agent named Sam, and he was looking at me with fear in his eyes.

"What the hell is going on?" he asked.

I said, "Sam, throw your apron in the corner of the joint and follow me! We got a 'Hey, Rube' going on and that means big trouble!"

Everybody was running toward the wheel. Sam and I joined them. When I got there, one of our bosses, Joe, was there to tell us all what to do next.

Joe screamed, "You women, grab your kids and hightail it to the trailers! You men, come with me to the entrance of the midway. That's where all the fighting is going on, and we're going for it!"

Different gangs were at different fairs. We were playing the Las Vegas fair at that time. Whenever we had trouble at the Las Vegas fair, it was always the Indian gangs who ruled this area.

The carnies were always ready for a fight. Women grabbed their children and ran for the trailers. The midway cleared out fast until all that was left were the angry men fighting.

When the police arrived, the carnies had everybody run off the midway. They were in physically good shape and tough. They believed in standing their ground. After all, this was their show—and you know the old saying, "The show must go on." We knew we were all we had, so we had to take care of ourselves. If we'd waited on the police, we all would've been dead by the time they had gotten here.

I was always scared when fighting and violence was happening. It triggered memories of my childhood when I ran to get help to stop my father from beating up my mom. It was always a nightmare at my house, which was filled with yelling and physical fighting when I was a child.

By the time I grabbed my son and got to the trailer in Vegas, I was pretty shook up. I was shaking all over! I could still hear the noise from the fighting but I felt safe being inside the trailer because there was a wall between the violence and us.

As things started to quiet down, I headed back onto the midway. Still shaking, I looked from one end of the midway to the other to make sure it was safe. I didn't hear any noise. Then I looked up and saw a bunch of Indians running like hell out the back way. I grabbed my son and ran back to the trailer, jumped in, and quickly locked the door. I prayed they would not come in.

After a few minutes, I heard a loud knock at the door and my body froze. The hair stood straight up on my arms. I wondered if I was going to have to shoot someone. I had my .38 pistol ready to go.

Then I heard Artie's strong voice. "Phyllis, everything is OK. You can come out now."

Artie always knocked before he entered. He was well aware of my fear of violence. He also knew I had a .38 and would use it.

It took me some time to calm down. Artie was the only one who could calm me down. His voice did that for me. He was my soul mate, my hero, and the man who took care of me.

Prologue

"Honey, I'm glad to hear it's all over," I said.

I couldn't have lived without my son, Brad, or Artie. They meant everything to me. They were my world.

I put my .38 back in the cabinet. I told Brad everything was going to be OK. And then with a smile on my face, I grabbed Artie and gave him a big kiss and hug. I was glad to know he was OK.

We all went back to work. If you hadn't been there an hour before, you wouldn't have known things had been upside down a short time earlier. Knowing everything was normal again felt good. Carnival music lilted from the merry-go-round and the Ferris wheel. The kiddy rides were busy and you could smell popcorn popping and corn dogs frying Everybody was eating cotton candy, drinking soda pop, and enjoying their hot dogs on a stick.

It was about noon, and it was very warm outside. The pavement was starting to look and feel like you could fry an egg on it. Soon the temperature reached 102 degrees. There was still a lot of day left, and we knew we would be hitting the showers the rest of the day, clothes and all. We had to stay cool so we could work in the heat. But business was as usual, and the rest of day went along well.

At night it started again. The Indians came back, and all hell broke lose. They started with the operator of the Tilt-a-Whirl. They walked up, pulled him off the ride, and five of them started beating on him. Luckily, Joe, who was on the Ring of Fire ride, saw the action and called, "Hey, Rube!" again. Everybody ran to the Ferris wheel and then to the Tilt-a-Whirl ride. I tried to run to the trailer after grabbing Brad, but I couldn't get through the crowd. So I had to stand there and watch the fight, which was the last thing I wanted to do. I really didn't want my son to see all the violence; I just wanted to get him into the trailer. Brad had always been told, like all the other carny kids, "If there is any fighting, run to momma right away, or run to the trailer, whichever is closest."

As I tried to get to the trailer, I looked through the crowd and I could see Tom, the ride jock they had beaten up. He looked pretty bad. He had blood all over him and was lying on the ground and not moving.

"God," I prayed, "please don't let him die. Please take care of him."

It was time to get out of there, but I couldn't move—I was frozen in fear. My heart was pounding so hard in my chest I thought it was going to explode, and I was sweating. Then I saw all the ride jocks jump in and start fighting the Indians, which were by now outnumbered. I could see bloody noses and blood all over the ground. The Indians weren't looking too good.

The other agents that worked in the joint arrived, and the Indians didn't have a chance. Luckily for the Indians, the police were close by and stopped all the fighting.

I was glad when that day was over, and I hoped we didn't have any more days like that one. We had two more days at that fair, but things went smoothly for the rest of the spot. Again, we had the police to thank. They took a few of the bad boys and put them in jail. That took care of that!

Needless to say, I was very glad when it was time to slough—tear down the show and get the hell out of town. It was a fun town with the casinos and all, but we were in a hurry to get going.

My blood still steams when I think of all those things that happened so long ago on the midway.

Prologue

The Carnival Girl

My son (age 2) and I in front of my balloon store in 1967 in an amusement park in Long Beach, California, called The Pike.

What Is a Carnival?

A CARNIVAL IS the annual celebration of life found in many countries of the world. Hundreds and hundreds of years ago the word *carnival* came from the followers of the Catholic Church in Italy. They started the holiday tradition with a wild costume festival right before the first day of Lent. Then as the French, Spanish, Portuguese, and Americans began to take control of other parts of the world, they brought with them their tradition of celebrating carnivals. *Carnival* means to free up your spirit, celebrate, party, costumes, dance, music, song, fun rides, cotton candy, snow cones, and hot dogs. Individuals come together to laugh, sing, dance, and celebrate.

    A traveling carnival is an amusement show that may be made up of amusement rides, food vendors, merchandise vendors, games of chance and skill, the acts, or sideshow curiosities. A traveling carnival is not set up as a permanent location like an amusement park, and is moved from place to place. Its roots are similar to the 19th century circus with both being set up in open fields near or in town and moving to a new location after a period of time. Unlike carnival celebrations or the European Funfair, the North American traveling carnival is not usually tied to a religious observance. Modern traveling carnivals play both state and county fairs, along with smaller venues such as church bazaars, volunteer fire-department fundraisers, and civic celebrations. Traditionally, on the evening of the carnival's last day, the sponsoring organization pays for a fireworks display signaling the end of the event.

Carnival Operations

Worldwide there are many different traveling carnival companies. Most carnivals are not made up of one operator of rides, food, or games. Many of these venues are operated by independent owners who contract (or "book") with the carnival. These independent owners are contracted to pay the carnival a percentage of what their rides or stands gross in sales. An owner of a large carnival will own a majority of the rides and games and book the rest of whatever he needs. Trucks transport most rides and games. Food stands are towed behind trucks or trailers. Some owners of large carnivals use rail to move their equipment for long-distance shows.

Carnival Games

Many traveling carnivals have games of chance and skill. Games like the crossbow shoot or balloon and darts test an individual's target-shooting ability. Other games such as the water gun game pit a group of individuals against each other to win the game. Chance is involved in games like the duck pond or the ping-pong ball and fishbowl game. Most games offer a prize to the winner. Prizes may be stuffed animals, toys, posters, or different games. Continued playing is encouraged to add up points for bigger prizes. More difficult games, including the baseball and basket or the stand-the-bottle game, offer a large prize after one win to any winner.

Most of the game operators run honest games. Some people still are wary of carnival games. This may be because carnival games in the past gained a reputation for being dishonest. It is interesting to note that the term *mark* (slang for "easy target") originated with the carnival. In many areas, local law enforcement officers would test the carnival games prior to and during the carnival to help eliminate rigged games. They would mark those that were not honestly operated.

Carnival Rides

Many traveling carnivals bring with them an assortment of rides. Some rides are for young children and may include a carousel, miniature railway, miniature roller coaster, or an inflatable bounce. There are also rides for older children and adults. There can be many different types of rides. These rides are designed to use fast speed and lots of motion for centrifugal force to appeal to riders' senses. Some examples are the Ferris wheel, Zipper, Chair-O-Planes, and the Tilt-a-Whirl. Carnival rides are painted in bright colors like red, yellow, and orange. State governments inspect carnival rides before the start of the show to ensure the safety for all rides.

Carnival Food

There are always food stands at carnivals. These independent concessionaires, like the independent ride owners, "book" their stands with the show's managers or owners. The food stands serve a variety of food and beverages. There are snack items such as cotton candy, ice cream, fried dough, candy, caramel apples, snow cones, hot dogs, and french fries. Beverages could include soda, coffee, tea, lemonade, and hot chocolate.

The Carnival Girl

Don Chapman (my husband) and I on The Pike in 1964.

CHAPTER 1

Growing Up Fast

I SEEM TO be doing a lot of daydreaming these days. In fact, I'm daydreaming right now! It is January 11, 2010, and I'm sitting in my comfy chair at my Coeur d'Alene, Idaho, home at the age of seventy years young. I'm watching the snow come down—and it's really coming down!

I couldn't have been doing much of anything on this day even if I had wanted to. In Idaho you hibernate when the snow is coming down this hard. As I'm looking out the window, I'm daydreaming about my life some fifty years ago as a carny, traveling with the shows each year.

How did I become part of the carnival life? My family had lots of love when we were small and we lived with Grandpa Jerry and Grandma Wilma. But somehow the love was lost along the way. Life was too much for my mom. I was sick of all the boyfriends, the drinking, and the boyfriends trying to get fresh with me when my mom wasn't around. I got tired of going to the bar to get something to eat after school and putting up with drunks.

In my fourteenth year on August 19, I was lying in bed on a Saturday morning thinking about the whole mess. I was fed up with it all. It was 102 degrees outside and 107 degrees inside the trailer, making me very miserable and wanting to run as far as I could. Nobody was home, which was nice for a change, so it gave me some time to think and make my plan to escape the trailer and my crazy life.

By then my mom was into the bottle, and we had no communication left. Eventually, I moved across the street to live with a lady and her three boys. I was a happy camper until her husband came home from the service. That's when the real trouble started.

He tried to get fresh with me. It seemed like everywhere I went, somebody was trying to go after me. I didn't understand at the time that it was really their problem. I was always thinking, *Where are their morals? Why are they thinking and acting like animals?* At that point in my life, I felt lost and scared. I had no idea how I was going to take care of myself. But I knew it was up to me.

My mother, Ruth, was born in Paris, Arkansas, in 1922. My sister, Raylene, was born in Tulsa, Oklahoma, in 1940. I was born in Leavenworth, Kansas, in 1942, and my brother, Ronnie, was born in New York City in 1946.

We moved every year from city to city and state to state. We attended a different school each year and sometimes two different schools in one year. My mom was like a born gypsy; she always thought the grass was greener on the other side. No wonder I felt right at home in the carnival, moving from city to city, and sometimes state to state.

My mom changed men like she changed cities. By the time I was ten years old, we kids had already had five different fathers. And that's just the ones she married! My Grandma Wilma used to say to me, "Phyllis, your mother has had more boyfriends and husbands then anyone I've ever seen."

I said, "Grandma, Mom said she was going to keep trying until she gets it right. Mom said if things are not good between two people in any relationship you need to just move on. Grandma, do you think that's how it's supposed to work? You move on?"

Grandma said, "Phyllis, your mom does move on quite a bit. I hope you don't live your life like your momma. You should try to work it out with the one you marry. Otherwise, you have to start all over again with the next one."

My mom and grandma did think differently about things. Me, I didn't know what to think. I guess you have to give my mom credit—she never did give up. She had the faith and spirit to keep looking for a good man and a good husband. All of that action might be the reason my sister, brother, and I have been single most of our lives.

We lived in an attic at Grandpa Jerry and Grandma Wilma's house in New York City. My mom said it was about 1,400 square feet. We had a kitchen, living room, bath, and one bedroom. There were five bedrooms on the second floor. That's where Raylene, Ronnie, and I had our bedrooms and their two guest rooms. My Grandpa Jerry and my Grandma Wilma lived on the first floor, where they had their own living room, kitchen, and one bedroom. That was in the days when parents, grandparents, children, and grandchildren all lived together. That's why they made the houses so big.

Things were pretty normal while we were living with our grandparents. We had lots of love and lots of good food. My Grandpa Jerry was Italian, so it was important for all of us to have our meals together and visit with each other. Dinner was the time to talk about everything that had gone on that day.

We loved New York City. There was always something happening and something new and different to do. We lived on a hill in the old part of town. All the houses were very big with big backyards. They lined up together street after street.

During the snowy season, my Grandma Wilma or my mom would be waiting at the door for us kids when we came home from school. We would walk about three-quarters of a mile to school and three-quarters of a mile home in the snow. My grandmother or my mom would always say, "Raylene and Phyllis, come in quick and let's get you dried off." They would put a nice warm blanket around us. Then my mom would say, "Now hurry over to the fireplace to get warm." They would hand us a nice cup of hot chocolate. Um-um, that was good.

The Carnival Girl

That's one of my great memories from New York City. That's how childhood goes—always some good memories and always some bad.

My siblings and I attended Catholic school and wore nice uniforms. I really liked most of my teachers, but sometimes they were a little strict. One morning I asked one of my teachers, Mrs. Anna, for permission to go to the restroom. Talk about memories! This is one I haven't forgotten. Mrs. Anna said no, that I could wait until after class. Well, that did not work out so well—I had an accident right there in my chair. I thought I was going to die, I was so embarrassed. The other kids looked at me and some laughed.

They called my mother to come pick me up, which didn't sit too well with her because she had to take time off from work. So then I was in trouble all the way around.

I wish I could forget some of my bad memories forever. I'm sure you have some of those memories from your childhood too.

After that, Mrs. Anna was pretty easy to get along with. She always said yes to me for whatever I asked. I would push it sometimes and go outside for a break because I could. I liked that school. They seemed to care about me and take care of me, and they tried to be very fair about everything. They made sure I was keeping up with the class work, and if I wasn't, they would help me until I did.

I loved the beautiful pictures of Jesus and Mary and the Last Supper. The stained-glass windows and the walls were full of beautiful pictures. I loved hearing the stories about Jesus and how things were during Bible times.

We always had a lot of activities going on—my mom would sign us up for everything. After school we had tap class two days a week. We had art classes and ice-skating classes. Then we had regular dance classes. My mom wanted to make sure we had a chance at everything. She really showed us a good time, and we loved every bit of it. We had a good mom.

We had a lot of fun and love in our childhood; I don't know where it went later on. I think hard times hit us and took some of those good, happy times away from us.

My Grandpa Jerry was born in New York City, and my Grandma Wilma was born in Arkansas. They were both kind and loving and lots of fun to be around. My Grandpa Jerry was always telling jokes and kidding around with us. Grandma was always baking cookies or cakes for us.

Most of the time my mom was home for dinner, except when she was working or looking for a new husband. In those days, looking for a husband was a top priority—women could not make it by themselves. They had to get married. My mom would say looking for a husband and a new father for us was a full-time job all by itself, but it was necessary for our survival.

I was a very adventurous child then. I thought I could be like Tarzan, so I climbed the telephone pole in our backyard. Then I started going across the wires, swinging from hand to hand yelling, "Tarzan is here!"

My mom saw me and started yelling, "Phyllis, go back! Phyllis, please go back!" I obeyed but I thought she was silly for worrying about me. I knew I could perform without a problem. I always felt like I lived in bondage, always being held down and never getting to do what I wanted to do.

We lived close to town so we could walk or take a bus to the movies or to go shopping. My mom walked to work every day. She was a waitress and always had a job in New York City.

In winter, she would say, 'Phyllis and Raylene, let's go sledding this weekend."

I would answer, "What have you been waiting on? I'm ready," and off we would go. That was one of my favorite things to do.

During the week, I would say, "Raylene, I will do your dishes tonight if you will go with me." Those were the magic words, and she always said yes."

Ronnie was four years younger than me. I remember him coming home from the hospital. But I was told at that time that he was my uncle.

Then I remember running down two flights of stairs screaming and crying my eyes out. I said, "Grandpa Jerry, come quick! He's doing it again! He's doing it again! Dad's beating up Mom!"

That time it was stepfather number two. Grandpa Jerry ran up to the attic where we lived and stopped him. He threw him out the front door. Grandpa called out at him to say he was a no-good Genie bum and to never comeback. I thought that was very strange because my Grandpa was a Genie, which was a slang word for an Italian.

But he did come back a few more times before it was completely over. I was six years old. I say it served him right. He was not a nice man; he would eat cookies in front of us and say that when we were good we could have some. I didn't know we were not good. I never understood what he meant.

He would come into my bedroom at night and do strange things to me. I was afraid to tell anybody because he was so mean. I started going into my sister's bedroom and hiding under her bed so he couldn't find me (or so I thought). I would sleep there or slip into my sister's bed and sleep with her. He finally left me alone. I'm sure he was afraid the truth would come out.

Ronnie and Raylene didn't like him either. My little brother was like my own kid. I did everything for him. I took care of him and he came to me for everything. I enjoyed being his caretaker.

The police were always being called no matter where we lived because my mom's husbands or boyfriends were always beating her up. Needless to say, we didn't stay in touch with any of them after the divorces. I guess none of the relationships were great.

Then, one morning as we were sitting at the kitchen table, my Grandpa said, "Phyllis, I've gotten a transfer and we're moving out of New York."

Grandpa said he always wanted to move out of New York. I think he wanted to get away from his family. Their last name was Malatesta, and they didn't have a good name in New York. They hung out with some rough people. Years later, I saw a movie about the Italian mafia, and the godfather's name was Malatesta. I don't know how real that was, but I always wondered. I asked one time and Grandpa laughed at me. Then there was a big silence that followed and we never talked about it again.

When I was sixteen years old and working, I realized how much he had done for all of us. I wanted to give him some kind of a gift in return. I asked Grandpa if he wanted to go back to visit his family and offered to pay for the trip to New York. Grandpa said, "Phyllis, thank you, but no. They are different people than we are, and they don't need to know where we are."

I asked, "Is there any other place you would like to go?"

He answered, "I'm happy right here, thanks again. I already had my gift. Being here together with my family is all I ever wanted."

What a message that was. It made me stop and think!

After that, we moved to Tulsa, Oklahoma. It was a beautiful, sunny day when we arrived. The temperature was about 75 degrees and Oklahoma was green and beautiful. We had a lot of relatives in Arkansas, which was close to where we were going.

"Mom, do any of them have horses, chickens, pigs, or cows?" I asked.

Mom answered, "Phyllis, you're going to see more animals than you've ever seen. And they even have a big, black bull."

"Mom, I can't wait to ride one of their horses. Do you think they will let me?"

"Yes, and they will teach you how to ride." I couldn't wait to get there! It was going to be lots of fun.

When we arrived, I met a lot of cousins. They took me and Raylene to meet their big, black bull. We went inside the fence to find him, and all of a sudden he appeared. Everybody started running and I followed them. We ended up hiding in the big red barn.

"Julie, what do we do now?" I asked.

Julie and Jake both spoke up and said, "We wait it out."

I sat on the straw with everybody else to wait it out, high up in that hot barn. It seemed like hours. Jake said if I was bored we could have sex. I told him no thanks but I was scared. I looked at Julie for support and she looked away.

Julie said, "Phyllis, you can do whatever you want." Again, I said no. I was hoping he would take me seriously, and thank God he did!

The Carnival Girl

My sister, Raylene, and I at the Oklahoma fishing hole. Raylene was age 10 and I was age 8.

Growing Up Fast

Two hours later as we were coming out of the barn, the black bull spotted us and charged. We ran toward the gate and I was happy when we got on the other side.

"Well, Phyllis, we got lucky this time," Jake said. "We outran that big, black bull."

"Jake, when did you not outrun him?" I asked.

"About a year ago. That crazy bull got me right in the butt. I wasn't running fast enough," he said.

"Yeah, Phyllis, he had to go to the doctor and get a few stitches right in his butt," Julie added.

I didn't think it sounded like a fun thing to do. I told myself to make sure I never played that game again.

"Jake, I would like to see your horses," I said. "Do you have any?"

Jake said, "Come along, Phyllis. We'll show you the horses."

Julie asked me if I knew how to ride. I didn't want to say no; I was afraid they wouldn't let me. It was all I had thought about as we were traveling across country from New York City to Oklahoma. It looked pretty easy in the movies and on TV.

"Yes, I can ride," I said. "It's been a while, but I can ride!"

I got on my horse and he took off running like crazy. I held on for dear life. Uncle Ivory had to get on another horse to bring me back. He laughed at me and said, "You fibbed, little girl. You never rode in your life."

I was busted and had to admit I had never ridden before.

"Uncle Ivory, will you teach me how to ride?" I asked. He said yes, and I was so happy. I got up at 7:00 a.m. to meet Uncle Ivory at the barn for my first lesson. I knew I was going to be a real cowgirl, after I learned how to ride. How excited I was.

The next morning, I got to go see the chickens. And I got to meet Uncle Luke.

"Phyllis, come with me and I'll show you the chickens," Uncle Luke said. He explained there were two different kinds of chickens; the ones that laid eggs and those that didn't.

"OK, that sounds like fun!" I said.

First we went to see the chicken that didn't lay eggs. All I could see were a bunch of skinny chickens tied to a short rope, connected to a stake in the ground. They had two pieces of wood shaped like a tee-pee and that was their home all year, rain or shine. They were called fighting cock chickens. This was big money in the South. I watched them fight and I thought it was disgusting. It was against the law, but I don't think anybody really cared.

The horses were the only thing I liked about the country—and, of course, all the good cooking. Country women know how to cook! I loved their homemade biscuits and sausage gravy, their fried chicken and mashed potatoes.

While we were in Oklahoma City, we got our first TV. It was so exciting! TVs had been out for a while, but we couldn't afford one until the price came down. The good part was we only had to pay for the TV—no monthly payments for cable like we have now.

It was about 1952. Our favorite TV show was *Howdy Doody* one hour each day. That must be hard to understand in today's world.

Everybody believed you would become like a robot if you watched TV too much. My mom was wise and wanted us to think for ourselves and use our own minds. Today TV is entertaining and relaxing for me. I can't imagine living without it.

Again we moved. Away from the country—no more animals, horseback riding, chasing the black bull, or watching the cockfights. We became city folks again. I quickly became bored, so every day after school I started building my own town in our backyard. I had lots of energy and I thought it would be fun to create my own private place. I dug a big hole and called it "Phyllis's World."

The hole was almost six feet wide and five feet deep. That was my first hole. Then I made a few other holes in the backyard. I was going to connect them together like little cities. I started digging tunnels but when my mother saw what I was doing she stopped me. She had been watching all along, but it was getting dangerous. That broke my heart.

"Phyllis, you have to cover all the holes back up," she said.

So there went the new world I was creating. Another disappointment.

One week later, a friend from school with whom I had helped dig a cave got smothered when a tunnel caved in. My God, that was a shock! That could have been me! My heart was broken for my little friend I would never see again. I would not be digging any more tunnels. I missed my friend Jim. I never have forgotten him.

Well now, it was time for my mother to work on husband number three, and she was going to Kansas City to do that. We stayed with Grandpa Jerry and Grandma Wilma again in Tulsa, Oklahoma. We stayed with our grandparents quite a bit between jobs and husbands, and we loved it. They were my most favorite people in the world. I always felt very loved and secure with them.

CHAPTER 2

Having Fun at the Carnival

LET'S GET BACK to my daydreaming! There's an unmistakable feeling of fun and excitement when the carnival comes to town. It's always great to hear the screaming and loud music coming from the midway and rides. Adults and children alike all have a great time. There are two rides the adults and children have always enjoyed the most: the merry-go-round and the Ferris wheel.

It's so good to see their smiling faces as they're buying their cotton candy and ice cream, not to mention buying their favorite corn dogs and elephant ears before they leave the midway and head for home.

It's a happy time for all because who doesn't love the carnival? The only thing different about our little town was it traveled on wheels as we made our living.

Everybody had a job and worked hard. Each had a responsibility, and it felt good to be working together for the same goals. Those goals were to make sure everybody had a good time at the show. We got up every morning and went to work, and we all loved being in show business. I know carnies have a bad name, but it's like anything else—one bad apple can create a bad name for everyone. There is good in everybody; it's there! Sometimes you have to look a little harder to find it, but it's there.

The Carnival Girl

Carnies are very hard-working people, so they don't have much time to get in trouble, and they are very good-hearted people. When the carnival came to town, the townspeople discovered their childhoods again, no matter what their age. We called our customers "marks" like you might call someone in your store a "customer." It's the same thing—a slang word.

As people made their way down the midways, strolling to their favorite game or ride, most of the hackers working in the joints would call to them to come and play their game of chance. They wanted you to win a big teddy bear or prize. My voice was always hoarse from calling out to everyone all day. I did my best to get people to come over to my joint and win a big bear. I worked a dart and balloon game, which is actually called a Hanky Panky joint. Somehow it's hard for the marks to resist the temptation of not taking a teddy bear, a fish in a bag, or something else home with them to show they were at the carnival having fun all day. After all, the carnival only comes around once a year.

A lot of people got into the carny business to be able to travel, and sometimes to follow the racetrack—the horse races. They would say they believed they were going to hit it big and get rich.

Some people were there for the fun and excitement that goes along with the carnival life. I got into traveling with the carnies because of my boyfriend.

A lot of the carnies were orphans who had no families. That made us all tight like one big, happy family. One minute you would see us fighting, and then the next minute we were loving each other like all other families.

Some people grow up in the same town and never leave. As a child I lived in New York, Texas, Oregon, Oklahoma, Kansas, Arkansas, and, of course, California. But I saw even more traveling around in the carnival. You travel a lot in the carny business, but you never have to pay rent, electricity, water, or a trash bill. You pay for your ride or game space you're renting for the five to fourteen days you're going to be working. When you worked in one of the booths, you were on commission and you were called a "jointee." If you worked for the show and sold tickets you were a ticket seller.

If you worked on one of the rides, you were called a "ride jock" and both of them were on a weekly salary.

When I was working in a booth, my only job was to make all the adults and kids smile and have fun. This brings out the side of the carnies so often overlooked. Most have amazingly big hearts, and it brings joy to them when they make people have a good time.

We saw all walks of life at the fairs we played. There were happy families, sad families, and young couples trying to win a teddy bear or some kind of prize. Sometimes people who were lonely just came to talk. Some came for a ride they loved, or because they had to win a teddy bear they'd been dreaming about for a long time.

Carnies often were running from the law or avoiding child support and had no place to go. They needed a job. Some people were drifters and found a home with the carnies. Some continued to be drifters. We also had 'lot lizards" looking for some kind of excitement and followed us everywhere—we were their addiction.

There were a lot of lessons to be learned from traveling with the carnival and being on the road for eight months out of the year. But all of that made me who I am today, and I like the person I am.

When the time came each year to end the season, we were all ready to take our four months off. By then we had played ourselves out with the traveling and all the hard work of setting up and taking down shows, including long hours and dealing with harsh weather.

I'm delighted to be telling this story about who carnival people really are. Carnies will do anything for you and help you out if they can. Most people didn't complain when they played my balloon game and walked away with a big teddy bear or some other prize. I tried to make them happy campers. They came to win a big prize and I came to entertain them and make some money. It was all in how much fun you made the game and how much fun the people had winning the prizes. If you entertained people in good fashion, they were always happy.

Once Artie said, "Phyllis, make sure all your customers win a nice prize for their loved ones. That will make them a hero, and everyone will go away happy and things will go smoothly."

Artie was the one who trained me how to work. I used to watch him before he became my boyfriend. Artie would take a $20 from a customer to play the game and he would give them a big prize like a big teddy bear, and they would walk away very happy. Artie had a way about him. He always entertained the customers and made the game a lot of fun.

If they were unhappy, he would give them their money back and then give them free tickets for other games so they could still try to win their teddy bear.

CHAPTER 3

Back to My Childhood

WHEN I WAS little, a scary thing happened. I suddenly couldn't walk—my legs had collapsed under me.

"Phyllis, the doctor said we have to put casts on both your legs for now, and when your bones catch up to your body in growth, we can take them off," my mom explained.

In those days they called it "growing pains" because they didn't know what it was. For eight months I wore those casts around my legs. The doctors tried to take them off at four months, but then said I wasn't ready.

After eight months they checked them again and found things to be normal and in good working order like they thought they would. Hallelujah! I was getting my legs back. I was getting tried of not being able to go outside and ride my bike and play with my friends.

My mom and sister were glad to hear the casts were coming off. When I was in the casts I had to use crutches, and was always falling. This kept my mom and sister busy always watching out for me. I'm sure they got tired of babysitting me, but it couldn't be helped. I also had a hard time sitting down on a chair or sitting on the bathroom toilet. My mom and sister had to each grab one leg for whatever move I was making, and then we would have to count, "One, two, three, OK, sit down now."

The Carnival Girl

    I would have loved to have lived with my grandparents for the rest of my childhood but it didn't work out.

    We knew our mom loved us, but she never had enough money or time for us. It was hard for women in those days; they didn't make as much money as men.

    We weren't rich, but we were not poor. Grandpa had a good job, and he took good care of all of us. We would stop at the local grocery store and charge an apple or a banana on the way to school and charge one on the way home each day. Grandpa Jerry had a charge account at the store, so we were the lucky kids in the neighborhood.

    We walked one mile to and from school every day and didn't think anything of it. It's what everybody did in those days. It's the way things were, and things went a lot slower in those times.

    My family knew all the people at the grocery store because they lived in the neighborhood. Jake, who worked at the store, lived across the street from us, and the owners lived one block away. The night-shift guy lived one block from the store, and the family who cleaned it lived next door to us. We were one big, happy family in one small town, and it was safe.

    Sometimes we would roam all over town. Mom or Grandma would give us a nickel once a week and we'd walk down to the candy store and have a great time. We could buy a lot of candy for that nickel!

    If my memory serves me right, the prices were a lot different in those days. That's when you could buy gasoline for ninety-nine cents a gallon and a newspaper for a nickel. You could watch a movie at a drive-in for thirty-five cents. The drive-in movie was a mile away and they had lots of chairs outside—not everybody had cars in those days. As a matter of fact, most people didn't have cars. If they did, there was only one per family and you drove it only when necessary. People still had horses to get around. It was a fun place to live.

    I enjoyed our time in Oklahoma. It was nice to have a lot of family around. But we were always moving around for one reason or another.

Grandpa Jerry was in the aircraft business, and there were factories all over. When he got another job transfer, we moved to Torrance, California, and took our rabbits and chickens with us. Grandma had to have her fresh chickens and rabbits along with fresh eggs! We had about twenty chickens and the cutest rabbits with their babies. We played with them all the time.

Back then, Torrance was like living in the country. After about twelve years they started building houses all around us—and there went our chickens and rabbits.

Eight years later when Grandma was dying, she told us Ronnie was our brother, not our uncle. What a shock that was! We had to adjust our minds completely.

Grandma would say things like, "Phyllis, it's about time to teach Ronnie how to ride a bike." She relied on me to help with my little brother because I was always around—and many times my mom wasn't.

I taught Ronnie how to ride a bike and how to box so he could take care of himself. And I took on the job of teaching him many other things. My mom used to say it was like he was my own little child. Since he was like a little brother to me, I was happy to finally know the truth.

By the time my mother married husband number four, my sister and I were fed up with these men trying to tell us what to do or attempt to get fresh with us. We wanted to leave and go anywhere they were not. We were ready to hit the road, but we had to figure out where to go.

It seemed like we were always on the move and running away.

CHAPTER 4

Back to Coeur d'Alene, Idaho, at Seventy Years Young

THESE DAYS MY mind tells me I'm forty or forty-five but my body tells me I'm seventy years old. Your mind has a way about it—it doesn't let you know you're changing and aging until you look in the mirror. You start to forget words and the direction you were going. They are in your mind, but instead of eventually coming out they stay there. You go from room to room to get something and by the time you get there, you can't remember what it was you were after. You go back to the room where you had the thought and pick up the energy—and then it comes back to you.

This works real good for me. I can always remember what I was doing; I just have to backtrack. I now know why you don't have all the time in the world when you retire—it takes two or three times as long to do things.

Sometimes I forget what day it is and sometimes I have to think hard to remember the new names in my family: wives, husbands, children, and dogs. Even though I have only one son, I have five grandchildren. One passed away at just sixteen—God called her home early. It was the saddest thing I have ever gone through, and we miss her a lot.

But God created miracles from her passing. My son and daughter-in-law donated my granddaughter's organs and saved eight other lives. I would say that was eight miracles, wouldn't you? Now I'm going on six great-grandchildren, and one is still inside her mommy's tummy. That will make it seven.

Sometimes I think life is very painful and I have to learn to deal with it, but then I have another great-grandchild and there comes another miracle. Life does go on, and I'm not keeping score or being ungrateful in any way. But at times I get scared when I wonder if this is the beginning of the end. It takes a long time before I admit to myself it is. But I know the good Lord has seen fit to bless me with another day, so I thank Him and keep on going.

> Brothers and sisters, I do not consider myself yet to have taken hold of it. But one thing I do: Forgetting what is behind and straining toward what is ahead, I press on toward the goal to win the prize for which God has called me heavenward in Christ Jesus.
>
> —Phil. 3:13–15

I'm sitting back in my lazy chair in Idaho again daydreaming about when my mother, my sister, and I lived in the trailer next door to my grandparents' house in Torrance. My mom was hitting the bottle pretty hard. I believe she was giving up on life and men.

We never saw much of her then. She would work all day and on the way home stop at the local bar, where she would spend her evening. There was never much food in the refrigerator, so sometimes I would go to my grandma's house next door to eat. My mom didn't like that because Grandma would know what was going on. She told me not to go anymore. So then I would have to go to the bar to get dinner every night after school. I didn't like the people who hung out there. They too would always try to get fresh with my sister and me.

My sister and I were again trying to figure out how we could live somewhere else. My brother didn't have to worry because he always lived with my grandparents.

What took me to on the path to my carnival days? When I was fourteen I took an entire bottle of my mother's diet pills. I knew where she kept them. I mixed them with some of the alcohol she hid in the trailer between the towels, under the kitchen cabinets, and on the shelf in the clothes closet. Then I wrote a note to my mother and the world.

In the letter I addressed my mother and told her how I felt much unloved and how she really only loved Raylene, who was the first child, and I being the second child was just in the way. She had already given away Ronnie, the third child.

Raylene had my mother's approval for anything she did or said, and nothing I did was ever approved. Either I said it wrong or I did it wrong. I had a lot of trouble in school while my sister did very well. It was hard to live with, always hearing how well she did and how I couldn't do the work. I had, I understand now, a disability called dyslexia, which means you see words and numbers backward or mixed and unmatched. It left me unable to do my schoolwork. So, of course, everybody thought I was stupid and my brain did not work properly.

I also talked to the world in my note. I said it didn't seem like a nice place to be and this was the right choice and I was happy to be leaving this mean world.

My mother came home and found my note and me. She screamed at me, asking me "why?" as she rushed me to the hospital.

When we arrived, they took me to the emergency room and put tubes down my throat, pumping out my stomach. It was horrible. My mother loved on me and said it was going to be different and that of course she loved all of us the same.

After we went home, that new mom lasted about a week until the weight of the world again became too much for my mother. She went back to the bottle and to not coming home after work, and I had to continue going to the bar for my dinner after school and putting up with all the drunks.

When my sister left home, I joined my mother in drinking. She let my boyfriend and her boyfriend move in with us. We started building an extra room outside our trailer with walls made of beer cans. It was warm in Torrance, so we could get away with living outside.

The Carnival Girl

One day my boyfriend's mother came over and had a fit. She made him move back home with his family. He was my first love. It felt like the world had come to an end again.

At fourteen I felt incapable of doing anything good or having any happiness in my life. This is when I moved across the street to babysit (after school) my neighbor Angie's three boys who were all under the age of twelve. She paid me room and board plus ten dollars a month. But this only lasted until her husband, Jake, tried to rape me.

"Susan, I'm so sorry but Jake tried to rape me last night," I told her. "He was wrestling with me, and then he started grabbing me in the wrong places and I told him to stop. I was really scared. Finally, I started screaming and he stopped. I got up and ran to my bedroom and locked my door."

Susan said, "Phyllis, I'm sorry I can't really believe that, not right now. I hope you understand."

I thought, *Sure, I understand. And I need to get the hell out of here right now.*

Jake had returned from being overseas for two years. He was serving his time in the Navy and had arrived in Long Beach, California, to stay there for two years. Susan and her children had moved there to be close to him. I'm sure she didn't want to hear what I had to say. Susan was very excited to have her husband home after two years, and her three boys were happy to have their daddy home. I did understand, and I knew I would be leaving as soon as I got my paycheck.

My sister moved across the street to babysit their little girl for ten dollars a month plus room and board. She also had a bad experience—they both wanted to have a party with her.

CHAPTER 5

Running Away to a New Life

FINALLY, MY SISTER, Raylene, and I moved out together to Long Beach. It was 1956, and I was fourteen and my sister was sixteen. We were excited about being on our way to a new life.

We moved to the YWCA. We thought nice girls lived there. But it didn't take us long to find out there were a lot of friendly girls living there who liked girls instead of boys.

We went to look for jobs at Taco Bell, the phone company, the electric company, McDonald's, Burger King, and a department store. We tried to find work at different offices in town and walked the pavement, going from store to store asking for a filing clerk job or whatever. We were discouraged; the YWCA wasn't working out and we couldn't find a job.

We were going to move out but that decision was made for us. Because we couldn't get a job, we were kicked out.

That's when my sister and I had to learn how to live under a bridge. It wasn't as dangerous in those days—at least that's what we thought. But we later found out differently. It was not safe. Our angels looked out for us and took care of us. Thank God! We were very blessed.

It was summer, and we had great imaginations, so we thought it was like camping out. That made it OK. We thought it was a lot of fun at first. Then we witnessed all the parties and fights happening at night on the beach.

The beach was an active place at night, and we found out that's where all the drinking and hard partying was. It turned out to be very dangerous where we were hanging out. We knew we had to move to get any sleep and to stay safe. We looked all along the beach and finally found a quiet, isolated area that could have been more dangerous—but we decided to take our chances.

This went on too long and we knew we needed to get an apartment to live a normal life again. We hadn't told anyone we were homeless; we didn't want anyone to know. They would have sent us back to our mom's, and that wasn't OK. We would have to make it work.

After about a month we finally found jobs at an amusement park called The Pike. It was a great amusement park on the beach that had carnival rides, cotton candy, corn dogs, and lots more. There were lots of sailors because we had a Navy base right next door.

We had found our new home and we were able to earn money. We could finally take care of ourselves and live on our own. But don't get me wrong—we had to work very hard.

All of our games opened at the same time every day—that was the rule. Our mornings started at nine a.m. and, with only one lunch break, went to ten p.m. on weekdays and midnight on weekends. We had to set up our game every morning because everything was put into the back room for safety reasons and the doors were locked at night. That meant we had to hang up all of the stuffed animals every morning on both sides of the walls in the concessions we worked that day.

If you worked in a balloon store (my favorite game), you got to work with all the kids, and they were always a lot of fun. You had to blow up all the balloons by mouth and hang them on the backboard. And you had to start all over again each time you had a customer. We kept a few extra boxes ready at all times. You also had to get your change ready, clean off the counters, and pull up the awning—then you were good to go.

Running Away to a New Life

The first game I ever worked was the basketball game. I had to sweep and mop the floors, hang up the animals, and get change ready, which sometimes meant running around the midway to get the right kind of change. The basketball game's owner never had the correct change to start. And then I had to open the awning, and I was ready to go for about eleven to fourteen hours.

You definitely had to be young and have a lot of energy to work in an amusement park. It took up almost the whole day just to have the job. That part really surprised me, but I accepted that even though I didn't like it. There was no time for a social life.

Long Beach was about fifty miles from Torrance, but what a different world. It was where all the runaways went. It was a sailor town, and you could get a job or a boyfriend there and survive.

But it was a rough town. There were apartments at the end of the amusement park called the Jungle—slums where everything in the world occurred: rape, robbery, and murder. Apartment after apartment was strung together like a maze. They had all been built in the early 1900s—about 1910. It didn't look like there were any building codes or rules at the time. The Jungle got its name right after the apartment projects were built.

My sister and I, plus two other girls, rented an apartment in the Jungle, and then after a while my sister and the two girls quit working. I had to take care of them and carry the ball.

When I applied for the basketball job, I met the owner, a little old man who was very weird. He colored his hair and mustache with what looked like a black marker pencil. He was as skinny as a light post and always had a cigar in the side of his mouth. He talked from the side of his mouth and always wore a hat. You could bank on seeing him looking the same way and having the same clothes every day—with that cigar hanging out of his mouth. But I took the job anyway. It didn't take long before he was trying to get fresh with me.

I was going to quit because he didn't know what "no" meant, and then the boss lady, Oral, who was the manager of the place, said, "Don't leave. I'll take care of this." He never bothered me again. I checked out my apron money with the boss lady every night. I never had to talk to him again; I would see him coming and going to pick up the money and that was all.

After I had been working at The Pike for about six months, I heard the boss man and his wife, Sally, were killed in a fire. Their bed caught fire from his cigar. He and his wife, who were always high on something, didn't hear the fire alarm go off.

When Oral bought the place, my job got easier. I didn't mind going to work at the basketball game anymore because I knew there wouldn't be any surprises. I wanted to do a good job. It was my first real job, not counting babysitting jobs back home. I wanted to keep this job. I had found out a job was a very important thing to have.

I met lots of different kinds of people. I met a lot of sailors and some Marines, but very few Army men. It was a sailor town without a doubt. I heard a lot of stories about their traveling trips overseas, and it sounded like it was a lot of fun. If I had been a man, I would have enlisted right then and there. But I was lucky I wasn't a man; I found out later things were not all so sweet in the service after all.

The Pike was the hangout for all the servicemen, and they were our main customers. Most of them were from back East. They were away from home, and that's how the service wanted it. They were told if any of them were momma's boys, they wouldn't be when they got done with them. Being away from home was part of their training.

I learned about the basketball game, a game of chance. But I was taught to sway my body to the right or the left to help them miss a little. I would stand in front or to the side and it would work most of the time. The owners said it was to help with the profit they would need to keep the store open and going since they didn't make much money. So to keep me working and getting paid I needed to sway a little—I didn't see any harm in it. Of course, I would have believed anything at that time of my life. I was very naive and didn't understand anything about business. All I wanted was to have a job to make enough money to pay my bills so I wouldn't have to go back home.

Lots of sailors asked to borrow some money from me. I always said yes and loaned it to them. I believed they were my friends. Most of them did not pay me back.

Oral said, "Phyllis, you ask them if you could borrow some money from them. After all, they are all your friends."

She wanted to turn it around so I could see clear—and clear I did see. I learned fast that only some of them would loan me money. A few said yes, and of course I paid them back.

The boss lady took real good care in looking out for me, and I didn't appreciate her enough. She also said I should get a place by myself so I wouldn't have to take care of anyone else but me. But as usual, being the kid I was, I didn't listen.

Finally, I quit too. I thought my roommates were having all the fun. They were meeting all the sailors, riding all the rides, playing all the games, and eating all the good food. I was afraid they were going to meet their true love and I wouldn't. We all wanted to have fun and fall in love and get married to have our own families. That's how we thought things were supposed to be. We were starry-eyed about life.

Well, it didn't take us long before our electric was turned off, which meant cold showers and no cooking.

This was not fun anymore, and none of us had found our true love or lived happily ever after. Before we got kicked out, we had a party every night and invited the sailors in. I would pass the hat to collect money for food for the next day. It kept us going. One of the girls knew how to cook, and we had a little gas stove so she would fix potatoes and beans—that's it. We were happy we were eating at all.

We had to go back to the bridge again. We kept one suitcase for ourselves, one blanket, one brush, one comb, and one change of clothes. The landlord kept everything else we owned. We would bury our suitcases in the sand in the daytime and pull everything out at night. *Oh, my God, we're homeless again,* I thought. But we knew what was waiting for us this time. We tried to stay out of the light from the roller coaster that shone its lights under the bridge.

We had to get way in the back where it was dark and scary, hoping nobody could see us.

One night we were sleeping under the bridge, and nine guys who were partying found us—and they had been drinking a lot. Oh, boy, we knew we were in a lot of trouble. We didn't know if they were going to beat us up or rape us or both, or if they were going to help us. It was very scary.

We told them we were waiting on our boyfriends and their friends because we were going to have a birthday party and that they should be there any time. We invited them—out of pure fear—to a make-believe birthday party. We were trying to act like everything was under control and things were good.

When we got up from the blankets we were sleeping on, one guy hollered out at us, "Hey! Don't bother getting up because you might be lying right back down again very soon."

We got very scared after that remark. We jumped to our feet, signaling each other to start running.

We then heard our boyfriends walking through the sand—we knew it was purely a miracle. We were surprised when we saw them walking over; their timing was perfect. They were definitely our angels that evening.

After that night, our boyfriends came to check on us or they would send some of their friends if they had duty. What a blessing that was. They would holler out to us, "We're here and the rest are coming." There weren't really any more coming, but they scared the troublemakers away.

There were a lot of good sailors in town who fought to keep us safe. They became our bodyguards each and every night.

One night our boyfriends were outnumbered and were definitely going to get beaten up. Luckily, they looked up and saw a big group of sailors hanging out a short distant from us. Our boyfriends called out to them and they came over.

Sailors had their own pact and stuck together. When one of them needed help they were there. Those sailors were our special angels that night.

Running Away to a New Life

We always came out OK because our angels were there for us. But we were learning a lot of big lessons along the way. Sometimes there were a lot of different sailors walking around on the beach at night we didn't know. At times they were very drunk and angry. Sometimes they were being nice to us and trying to protect us. We never knew what to expect. Our boyfriends tried to help us get an apartment or at least find somewhere we could clean up.

We knew a lot of people on The Pike, so we didn't have too hard of a time borrowing somebody's shower. But we had been on the beach for too long without jobs or food. How had this had happened to us again?

Then a bell went off in our heads. Cause and effect: if you don't pay the rent, you won't have a place to live. This went on for about three months, and we really learned a new lesson or two. Sometimes you have to get hit in the head to grow up and learn, and grow up we did. That was our last time under the bridge. I learned to respect my job more and worked hard to keep it.

I'm sure if we didn't live in a sailor town, we would have gone hungry. Sometimes we would ask different sailors to buy us breakfast or dinner. They would sometimes ask us to lie down for them, and we would say yes. After we ate we would sneak out the bathroom window from the restaurant and run away. I know it wasn't a nice thing to do, but we didn't know what to do—we were very hungry. In those days men treated most all women with respect unless you gave them a reason not to. Just because we were homeless didn't mean we were bad girls; it meant we were girls in trouble.

Most all the sailors wanted to help us, and there were only a few who wanted to take advantage of us. With all of our troubles, we were still nice girls. Our mom had taught us if you didn't stay a virgin, nobody would marry you.

One day the ballgame was suddenly over. The police came and took my sister and me home to our mom. Things were different in those days—you could go to jail for just running away from home.

The next day, I asked my mom's boyfriend if he would take me to the bus station. He said yes, and he did just that. He wanted me

The Carnival Girl

gone as much as I wanted to be gone. So I went right back to The Pike to get my job back. Luckily, I did.

My sister found a boyfriend who was of age to take care of her, and she left home again.

I had made friends with two girls from Indiana: Sue and Mary. They had come to stay with their aunt in Long Beach. Sue was unwed and having a baby, so she had to be sent out of her town until the baby was born. An unwed pregnancy was unheard of in those days. There were different schools or homes to send these girls so nobody would see them or know about their pregnancy. They were expected to place their babies for adoption or find a relative to whom to give their babies—even if they didn't want to. It was definitely the way of the times; that was one of the worst sins you could ever do.

When Sue's baby was born, it was time for them to go home. The police were looking for me again, so I asked Sue if I could go with her. She agreed, and we took the train back to Indiana. Back then, people traveled by train because airplanes were only for the rich.

Train rides were actually fun; you could play cards and meet a lot of different people in the dining car. Passengers ate their dinners in the dining car and hung out there for most of the ride. They served cocktails, breakfast, lunch, and dinner, and I really enjoyed the food.

I was happy about another chance at life until I met Sue's parents. They weren't happy to see me—I was a surprise to them. I didn't know Sue and Mary lived with their parents. They also had a brother my age. I stayed a while and he started to like me. Eventually we started going together.

Sue got jealous and called the police on me. I was headed back to Torrance, California—again.

CHAPTER 6

Getting Out of Jail

I WAS IN jail for thirty days in Indiana while the police made arrangements to send me home. They didn't seem to be in a hurry. My cell had one bed, four walls, and one toilet. That's all I could see all day, although there was a window up high that allowed some light in my cell.

Three times a day somebody would come to feed me but that was it. They only stayed long enough to give me my food, and they didn't talk to me. The food wasn't bad. The sheriff's wife cooked the meals in those days, and the food was passed through a little gate with a small slot.

You would have thought I was a real criminal. Isolation was part of the lesson I was getting that time around. I was in solitary for thirty days and didn't know it. It was real tough.

After a while, I found myself talking to the birds outside my window. I could hear them making different sounds, and I thought they were answering me. The four walls were getting to me. Then I heard a voice talking to me, a real live voice from the other side of the wall. There was a wire fence between us. I couldn't see anybody—I could only hear his voice.

The Carnival Girl

He said he was in the next cell and had arrived the previous night, arrested for fighting. That was another blessing for me because I was losing it with four walls and nothing to do all day.

I realized he could see me in my cell when I was sleeping, talking to the birds, and going to the bathroom. I thought I was going to die, but I still could not see him. I wondered if there was really a jailbird talking to me or if it was the sheriff talking to me.

He wanted to talk about sex, and I said I wouldn't talk to him anymore if he didn't stop being rude. He finally showed me some respect and said he wouldn't talk about sex. We talked about our families and where he had been in his life. He said he had done a lot of traveling overseas in his days while he was in the service. It sounded like a lot of excitement and fun. I always wanted to travel.

We talked on and off during the days, and it kept my sanity. I had to wait for him to say hello first. I tried to talk to him other times but he wouldn't answer. That's why I thought it was the sheriff to whom I was talking.

The jail I was in was old, and it looked like it only had one or two cells. It wasn't busy; I was the only one there for thirty days, not counting the so-called guy on the other side of the wall.

Finally, arrangements were made, and it was time to go home. I was glad to hear the news—I was ready to get out of jail.

I was put on a train, but the first chance I got I jumped off. I was running away again. But they picked me up and the sheriff said, "I told you to get out of my county."

I was a real sad little girl; I guess I wasn't listening very well. So I went back to jail. The next time they put me on a plane and handcuffed me. It was embarrassing and humiliating. You would have thought I was a real criminal.

When I arrived in Los Angles they delivered me to juvenile hall. It was a jail for underage kids. My mother signed me away for two years to the court system. She said she couldn't control me and they said they could. The policewomen in the jailhouse said to me, "Ha, ha, you're ours for two years. Get ready to be a good listener and a good worker."

Getting Out of Jail

I was scared to death. I wasn't sure what I had gotten myself into this time.

It was not fun in jail. Other inmates would steal my food and tell me to shut up about it even though the food was nothing to talk about. I lost about twenty pounds in four months. I was already skinny—after jail I was a beanpole.

Inmates would call me names, shove me around, and talk about raping me, although it never happened, thank God. After four months, my grandma came to get me out, although we had to go to court for that to happen. The court day was scary. I didn't know if I was going to go home or not. The judge made my grandma promise to keep me at home and in line.

We told the judge I would stay home until I was eighteen years old. The judge insisted I needed to live with my grandma, but again there was no room. She only had a two-bedroom home, and my brother already lived with her. My mom and her boyfriend were now occupying the trailer where my mom, sister, and I had lived. It was only about twenty feet long—not big enough for all of us—but I had to move in there. My sister and I told my mom we had voted no more of her boyfriends could live in our home again. She didn't care—she said we didn't have a vote and that she needed his income to make ends meet.

I was always finding liquor bottles hidden around the house. For example, I would reach for a bath towel and find a bottle between the towels, or I would find them in the cabinets or in the closets. My sister and I were not surprised Mom had picked her man and liquor over us.

Raylene and I soon decided to leave home again. Raylene just went away with some of her friends that she knew. I had already lived on my own and I liked it a lot better. I couldn't bear living with my mom or grandma again and having to revert back to being a kid. I really wanted to be on my own and pay my own way. I knew I would be OK if they would all let me be.

The morning of my departure I went to my grandma's house and gave her lots of hugs and kisses. I thanked her and told her I loved her very much, but that I had to leave and not to worry.

She said, "Phyllis, please stay out of trouble and be careful and remember Grandma always loves you."

"Grandma, I'm going back to The Pike to get a job, and I will be able to take care of myself, not to worry," I said. "Grandma, you are my favorite person in the world. I really love you and I won't let you down, I promise."

We hugged again, gave each other another kiss, and I said, "I love you. Bye for now, Grandma."

I asked my mother's boyfriend to help me run away again. This time he gave me twenty dollars and drove me to the bus station.

"Take it easy and good luck," he said as I got out of the car.

I made it back to The Pike and got my job back. But the police remembered me, and I knew they were going to pick me up again, so I started making plans to leave. I had an address for another friend I had met in Long Beach who had gone home to Missouri. We seemed to get along well, so I decided that was where I should go next.

CHAPTER 7

I Booked a Train Ride to St. Louis, Missouri

I WAS NOW sixteen years old, but still looked about fourteen. Once again I was excited to think about starting a new life. I was imagining everything would work out for good.

When I arrived in St. Louis, I got off the train and a guy hollered at me, "Taxi, lady?" He ran over and grabbed my bags, helping me into the cab.

He asked where I would like to go. I handed him my friend's address and told him I was going to surprise her.

That was the wrong thing to say.

The driver took me across town to a rundown neighborhood, stopping at a motel. When I saw where we were, I got real nervous.

He stopped the cab, grabbed my bags, and started going inside.

"Come with me," he called.

I got out of the cab and went into the motel. He had already checked me in.

"What about the address I gave you?" I asked.

"We'll get there in the morning. It's too late now," he said. I trusted him and thought my friend's house was indeed far away.

Someone else took my bags, and I followed this guy to the fourth floor. He took me inside a motel room and then left. I quickly

The Carnival Girl

locked the door, but within seconds somebody was trying to get into my room. I was getting worried about where I had ended up.

I looked out the window and said, "Oh, my God!" All I saw were black people. Black and white people did not mix in those days.

Whoever was trying to get into my room found the door locked, so he started knocking. When the knocking stopped, I grabbed my bags and went to the motel's back door, ran down the stairs, and just kept running. I ran three blocks down the road—I knew I had to move fast, because it was getting dark.

I saw a white driver in a yellow cab, and I said, "Please help me. I will pay you if you will take me to my girlfriend's address." I told him that's where my money was, and he said yes. But I didn't really have any money—I'd used it all for the train rides.

It wasn't very far; it only took us about fifteen minutes to get there. When we arrived, I got out of the cab and told him I was sorry and that I didn't have any money but that when I got a job I would pay him.

He was mad and started screaming at me. Scared and panicky, I ran up the steps and found my friend's apartment. I started banging on her door. She opened it, and I said, "Surprise!" and jumped inside and slammed and locked the door.

What a hello that was! The cab driver banged on the door for a while and said the least I could do was give him a "party." We didn't answer, and he finally went away.

That was sure scary. I didn't want to ever go through that again.

I was lucky my friend still lived in that apartment. She could have moved, and I would have never known. And then where would I have been? I would have gotten myself in trouble all over again.

I still had a lot of faith. I was on my way to a new life once again.

It took a while to get a job. Again, nobody wanted to hire me. I looked young and like I might have been a runaway, but I wasn't going to tell anyone. I knew they would call the police, and I would go back to jail.

I Booked a Train Ride to St. Louis, Missouri

When I finally got a job after looking for two and a half months, my girlfriend wanted me to move out—if I could even call her my girlfriend anymore. I'm sure she was tired of feeding me and taking care of me. She explained she wanted me to move out because her boyfriend was going to move in. He was going to be helping her with the rent and expenses. I understood.

I was working in Illinois, in a place called East St. Louis, across the state border. I asked my new boss if he knew of any apartments close by. The boss said I could live upstairs from the bar where I was going to work. I had no car, so that would work perfectly. But I found out later the six rooms upstairs were where the "girls" lived—it was a bordello, an old whorehouse! The good news was, no men were allowed up there then. At least I had somewhere to live.

Even though I was only sixteen and working at a bar, the customers didn't care—anything went in East St. Louis. Later, I was told I had to start asking the customers to buy me shots of alcohol at the bar. I had never drunk hard liquor before, but I did what I was told. I wanted to keep my job.

The drinking was a disaster—I couldn't drink hard liquor. I passed out behind the bar every night. My boss had to help me upstairs to my room every night. Yet I still had to continue asking customers to buy me a drink.

After six months, my boss said, "Phyllis, you never go out with anyone and you don't go dancing. And you don't do anything except work. You can't handle drinking, which is part of this job. You don't belong here. I need to call your mom and tell her you're coming home."

He then paid for my ticket and sent me home. My mom was happy to know I was OK.

CHAPTER 8

The Pike and Getting Married

AGAIN I WENT back to The Pike to get a job. I was tired of running when all I wanted to do was make my own way in life. I looked around to find a sailor who would marry me. That way I knew I would be legally independent.

I got lucky and found one.

The sailor I met was leaving to go overseas to Germany for two years. It was perfect for me. I could be on my own and I would even get a small check each month. We didn't love each other, but he thought it would be nice to have someone back home waiting for him. So together we thought this was a good idea.

A new life—again! I had faith and was ready to go for it.

I was sixteen, and the life lessons were adding up. By this time I had been beaten up and raped a couple of times in between all my moving from place to place.

A lot of things can happen to you when you leave home early. There is definitely a reason why you should wait until you are eighteen-plus—you don't have enough common sense and don't know how to take care of yourself before then. Life is what decisions you make and how you make them. If you make the wrong ones, you pay for them one way or another.

I always thought there was a higher power running my life. I would pray, "Lord, what is it I'm supposed to get out of this lesson? I hope I got it. Or am I going to get it right away and not have to repeat any of these lessons again? I'm trying to pay attention so I can move on to the good things that are coming my way in my life."

I thought things were going to get better once I was back at The Pike and had my old job back. But I didn't stay at The Pike for long. Family affairs came up for me, and I had to move on again.

CHAPTER 9

Indian Country

ONE DAY MY mother, who had just divorced husband number five, came over and said my uncle needed us because his wife had just died and his son had died six months earlier. He was feeling pretty low and needed some family.

So we packed up and we went to Beatty, Oregon, to visit my Uncle Russ and the Klamath Indians. Uncle Russ lived on the reservation with the Indians.

I remember thinking my Uncle Russ was one of the best people I had ever met, especially for being a man. He had come to visit us when I was very young, and he had seemed like a nice person. I was leery of men because they had treated me bad and destroyed my childhood. Now that I was an adult, I saw him through different eyes. It took me a long time to find out there were a lot of good men in this world, and they actually treated women well.

Uncle Russ was a drinker like my mom, and I was surely working on being a big drinker.

My brother took the trip with us. He was only fourteen years old but was getting in trouble in school, so my grandma said, "Go with them, and you can learn how to behave and learn something."

My grandparents had spoiled him too much, so he didn't like taking orders from anyone. He was kind of young, but we were glad to have him aboard. He ended up being our driver most of the time.

Grandma had said, "Ronnie, you could learn to work and pay your way in life." If she only knew our life was going to be wild and crazy. But none of us knew, really. Maybe only my Uncle Russ knew how things were going to turn out.

Grandma was always looking out for us. She was our caregiver until she gave me the job for the whole family.

When we were in Klamath Falls, in a restaurant or bar, I would slip my brother some booze out the back door when nobody was watching, or I would slip him a drink from my glass. I had no idea it was bad for him or me; it was what you did when you were an adult. We were being treated like adults and thought we were lucky to be living the life we were.

We had no idea we were killing ourselves or setting ourselves up for poor health in the future. Our drinking was affecting our liver, heart, kidneys, and everything else in our bodies. The bars were serving me, even though I wasn't old enough. They didn't care much in those days—if I had the green, everything was OK.

Uncle Russ's two sons were half Klamath Indian. The Klamath had sold their reservation to the government in 1961, so my uncle had received a lot of money, although it took forever to complete the transaction, and it was 1974 by the time the Indians got all their money. The government kept putting off paying the Indians their balance, so the Indians had to fight for what was coming to them.

The land the Klamath sold is in Winema National Forest and is still beautiful. There are beautiful lakes and rivers, and you can actually see the bottoms of the rivers and streams. The incredibly blue, clear water is truly inspiring.

Klamath County, Oregon, is the home of Crater Lake National Park and it is located east of the Cascade Mountains and north of the Oregon/California border. The basin hosts the largest number of wintering bald eagles in the lower forty-eight states. They begin arriving in November of each year.

During the spring and fall bird migrations, you can see thousands of Canadian geese, pintails, mallards, cormorants, gulls, herons, pelicans, and other marsh birds and waterfowl. That area has some of the best hunting and fishing on the planet.

Uncle Russ and the Indians lived off the land for a long time. The Indians got to enjoy it all year round and didn't need any hunting tags.

I got a chance to meet my uncle's Indian friends. They were very wild. I had a lot of fun, at first.

My uncle was a hero in the rodeo. He did everything and won often. He was a rodeo champ and knew everybody in the towns of Beatty and Bly, which were in the middle of the Klamath Indian Reservation near Klamath Falls. He was as wild as the Indians but was very protective of us. We had no responsibilities—no cooking, no cleaning, and we would eat out for breakfast, lunch, and dinner. We would take our clothes to the laundry and have them washed for us.

We learned a lot about people. Our life there was like a school for understanding people. Our communication skills were improving all the time. We got to listen in on Uncle Russ putting together business deals at least twelve different times.

That year we sold Christmas trees for a while. My brother and I stayed on the lot in a little trailer to keep people from stealing things at night. My mom and Uncle Russ got their own motel rooms, and we would go over in the daytime to take a shower. The trees were from the reservation, and we got them for free. They were fresh, beautiful, and fragrant.

There was a bar across the street, and that's where Uncle Russ and my mom were most of the time. I was too young to go by myself. So I hung out with my brother, and we stayed on the tree lot. We sold most of them. Buying and selling Christmas trees made us a lot of money—but it didn't last long enough.

When the tree lot ended, we went to stay in my uncle's house in Beatty on the reservation. I didn't get much sleep at that house. There were rats there—not mice but rats as big as dogs or cats. They ran around on the floor right in front of you!

There were dead rats in the toilet. They would drown themselves trying to get a drink of water. It scared me to death. I would have to call Uncle Russ to clean out the rats from the toilet before I could use it.

My uncle had built the Beatty home for his first wife. I was glad when we got to move to his house in Bly, a bigger, nicer house. My uncle had built this home for his second wife, the one who had just passed away.

There were two sheriffs in town—one wouldn't drive over fifty-five miles per hour and the other one went home by six every night. So the people ran the town. There was nothing tame about it. As the old saying goes, "The strong will control and survive." It was the Wild West there, without a doubt.

Some things that went on in town I'll never forget. One night we were in a bar in Beatty, about twenty miles from Bly and another twenty miles from Klamath Falls. Beatty was in the middle of the Klamath Falls Reservation. When I saw a fight going on outside one of the local bars, I went to see what was going on. One of the men had pulled out a knife and had started stabbing the other guy. The other guy was lying on the ground not moving.

I believe he was dead. And nobody did anything about it. Nobody tried to stop the fight. They watched the whole thing and walked away. I'd never seen anything like it. Nobody called the police. I was told to walk away like everybody else did.

The next morning I saw a story in the newspaper about a casualty in the parking lot of one of the local bars in town. There was no other information and nobody talked about it again.

I became fearful. *My God,* I thought, *is this how things are handled around here? Please help us.*

I guess these things happened all the time around there, but not in my world. I wanted to go back to California. I tried to stay drunk so I wouldn't think about what I was seeing again and again. Everybody else went on like it was a regular day after these incidents, yet it was all pretty shocking. I saw person after person get beaten up, and nobody did anything. In California the fights were stopped. I was used to people being more sensible.

The Indians had their own laws: take care of yourself and mind your own business. If you were big enough to get in trouble, you were big enough to take care of yourself. They warned you to stay out of other people's business or you would get the same.

They also had a strange way of thinking about death. The Indian women would go off for the last couple of years to live by themselves so they could die alone. They said when it was their time, it was their time. I asked the Indian men what they thought, and they said that was their custom. End of discussion.

One night, my uncle got beat up, and the next night my mom got beat up. All they had done was disagree with somebody in the bar. I tried to stop both fights, but a great big Indian picked me up and held me in the air while I was screaming and kicking. I had to watch the whole thing. It was painful to watch my mother and uncle get beat up and not be able to help them.

You couldn't be out in town at night—anything could happen.

The Indian families had all that Indian money and didn't know what to do with it. They bought new homes and played football in the middle of the living room. They were not used to having money or new cars and nice homes.

One night my uncle said, "Let's go and visit one of my best friend and relatives, Junior, who lives in Beatty." He had a brand-new three-bedroom, two-bath house that was pretty nice.

When we went inside, they had a fire burning right in the middle of the living room. They could have burned down the house! And maybe they did. We didn't stay long because they were drinking, and my uncle said it might get a little wild.

These people were always getting drunk and wrecking their new cars. They would just go and buy more. They would tear up their homes, and go and buy more houses. They thought the money would never run out. They had a lot of money, but they didn't know any better, and there was no one to educate them.

Many would go into the bars and have fights. They'd destroy the bar and then pay the owner for the damages. The next night, they would go back and do the same thing again in the same bar. It's like they really didn't know what to do with their time and money except drink and fight. Some partying, huh?

The rumor about Indians not being able to hold their liquor was certainly true. The day after drinking, they would not remember what the heck they did the night before. They beat their wives and children because they thought that's the way things were supposed to be.

When I was a little kid and my Uncle Russ and his wife, Janet, came to visit us in Long Beach, I overheard my uncle slapping around my Auntie Janet in the bedroom. It really upset me, and when he came out of the bedroom, I was old enough to ask him why he was hitting her. Uncle Russ said men have to do that sometimes. He said he didn't like to, but he had to keep her in line.

I spoke up and said, "Uncle Russ, you don't have to, and you shouldn't do that to someone you are supposed to love."

I got in a lot of trouble from my mother, who said, "Phyllis, keep your two cents out of their business." But I was glad I had said it anyway.

I think they were definitely very backward in all their ways. It felt like I was going back about fifty years in time when I was around them.

Sometimes Uncle Russ would have to stand guard for me when I wanted to go to the restroom at the local bar or restaurant in Beatty. If he didn't, one of the male Indians would walk in because he wanted to, whether you liked it or not. They were used to doing and saying whatever they wanted on their reservation. And nobody was going to stop them, unless you wanted to get hurt or possibly get killed.

One day at the restaurant I walked by the Indians to go to the restroom, and they decided to pull me into their booth. They wouldn't let me get up. I tried a few times, and then I called for my Uncle Russ. He came over. But there were four of them and only one Uncle Russ.

I was so nervous about the whole thing! Uncle Russ started talking to them in some kind of different language and it went on for about five minutes. It sounded like Uncle Russ was saying the same thing over and over. I didn't have any idea what he was saying.

I wondered if I was being sold, or if they were trying to buy me. My mind was going crazy. I didn't know where I stood in this fight or how things were going to end. I did know women didn't have any say around those parts.

Uncle Russ told me later it was Indian talk he had been speaking. He said he told them I belonged to him. Luckily, he knew them all, so when he told them I was his property they let me up from their booth. They stood up and shook Uncle Russ's hand, and then I walked away with my uncle. I didn't mind being my Uncle Russ's property as long as it got me away from those wild Indians.

You know the old saying that you have to pick your battles wisely? This was one of those times. I was so glad I had my Uncle Russ fighting the battle for me.

It was like nothing I'd ever seen—like something you would see in the movies, not in real life. I understood if and when the Indians decided they wanted to take me out back for whatever pleasure they wanted, nobody would be able to stop them. I found myself praying, *Please, God, take me back home to California where I will be safe.*

In California, women had more rights and were getting more all the time. In this part of rural Oregon, men were in charge whether you liked it or not. It was one more thing that scared me. That's how it was in my childhood.

Before the sale of the reservation, the Indians lived off the land like they had done for centuries. The only work they had to do each day was hunt for food and grow their own vegetables. They seemed nice when they were sober, and they had loving, caring families just as we did.

A few decades earlier, the Indians had lived in caves, and my uncle had lived there with his wife and three boys. Uncle Russ showed me the caves where they lived. I thought the whole thing was unbelievable, but he said it was true. They spent most of their days hunting, loving, eating, having babies, and enjoying their freedom. That was before the white man started controlling them. Then they had to start working hard every day like the white man, mostly logging. They started drinking, and they had nothing to bring joy and pride into their lives anymore.

Indians were the keepers of the land below their feet. Before the white man took over, the Indians were very spiritual and loved the land, and they gave back to the land where they lived and enjoyed their freedom at the same time.

The Klamath tribes had always lived in the Klamath Basin of Oregon. Their legends and history tell how they think the world and animals were created and how the creator sat together with the animals and discussed man's creation. The tribe's mission was to protect, preserve, and enhance the spiritual, cultural, and physical values and resources of the Klamath, Modoc, and Tahooskin people and the well being of the homeland for those who abided there.

It was great to see the joy and fun they were having with the money they received from the sale of their reservation. They certainly deserved it—it was about time and I'm sure well appreciated.

I sadly wondered what they were going to do when their money was gone, though. They were not accustomed to our ways; it was not going to be a pretty picture. I was disturbed over what was going to happen to them.

I wish I could have helped them in some way. I knew it was going to be painful for them. It's not fun to see the writing on the wall and know you can't do anything about it. But I had to go on with our plans of trying to find a bar to buy with the Indian money my uncle had received.

CHAPTER 10

Leaving the Reservation

IT WAS TIME to hit the road again. Uncle Russ was antsy and wanted to get going.

"Phyllis, this money is burning a hole in my pocket," Uncle Russ said.

We left the reservation and started traveling around Oregon looking for a bar.

"We might as well party a bit while we are looking," he said.

"Uncle Russ, I think that's a good idea," I said.

We drank every day for eight months, moving from town to town. We were looking for the perfect bar or bar and restaurant combo. Of course, I was very agreeable with anything my Uncle Russ had to say. My life was going pretty easy compared to where I had come from. I was happy not to be working myself to the bone just to survive.

I felt safe with Uncle Russ for the first time in a long time. I was taking a break from life as if my Uncle Russ was giving me a vacation. He was taking us on a big ride, and it was educational, exciting, and different. I certainly didn't have anything else to do!

We went to a few resorts and many towns as we traveled Oregon. The first resort we went to see was in between Myrtle Creek and Grants Pass off of Highway 5. There was a bar, restaurant, motel, and post office on the property. It was a cute little country town surrounded by beautiful green pine trees, and there was a river in walking distance. It was a picture-perfect scene anyone would be lucky to experience.

We stayed at this resort for two weeks. We liked it there—we were more like vacationers then people looking to buy real estate. We went fishing for a few days and did a lot of hanging out at the river, swimming and bathing in the sun.

We took great walks through the forest. I was getting acquainted with nature for the first time in my life—I had lived in the city most of my adult life. I know I would like to live there someday, because it was quiet and peaceful. I could actually hear myself think. This was way different then city living.

I told my uncle I would like to live there, but he said we couldn't put the money together and would have to move on. I wished my uncle would have changed his mind and bought that place. But I found out later we really couldn't afford it. I really didn't know anything about business.

We finely gave up on Oregon and started looking in California.

We made it to Red Bluff, California, and stayed there for ten days. Nothing felt right. We checked out many bar and restaurant combos, a few bars, and one motel. We tried for a few more days but nothing fit our budget. We searched local newspapers and talked to a couple of real estate agents but found nothing. The people didn't seem friendly either—maybe that was because it was too different after being in Oregon where the people were very friendly.

After breakfast one morning, Uncle Russ said it was time to hit the road again. When he had awaken that morning he had a good idea to go south and things would work out for us. He said we were checking out of the motel and told me to pack my things.

Uncle Russ said he had a dream about going south and we'd find our destiny. He traveled off Highway 5 to Woodland, California. It was a nice town, and the people seemed friendly. We had to stop there for gas, and then we had some bacon and eggs. The breakfast was fresh, and the bread was homemade.

Leaving the Reservation

My uncle was always talking in riddles—straight talk was hard for him. You had to learn to read between the lines, but you never had to worry. He was a kind and loving man. I loved him like the father I never had, and I respected him for his knowledge and how well he took care of us. I really did appreciate him, and he turned out to be one of my best friends.

We stayed in Woodland for two days, but there wasn't anything for sale that looked good for us. The properties were either too much money or they needed too much of a down payment.

We finally found a place in Hawthorne, California, on Crenshaw Boulevard close to the Army base. It was also close to Torrance in a busy part of town. There were lots of people, and that's what we were looking for—the more people, the better the business.

My uncle said this was a very good deal. It was a military town with lots of young families and lots of people. He said, "Phyllis, we have found the one." My uncle bought the bar.

My mom liked it, and my brother and I were happy. But I knew I wouldn't want to live there a long time. I was still thinking about the country setting I had seen on the road and wanted to return to some day.

Still, this was going to be my first business adventure, and I really wanted it to work. I was going to do everything I could to make that happen. My uncle said the business belonged to all of us and we would be sharing in the responsibilities. We were business partners, and that was a big motivation for me and gave me a good reason to work hard. I worked behind the bar and served beer and wine to everyone. I was the top bartender.

Nobody knew I was only seventeen years old. I told them I was twenty-one, and they settled for my answer. My uncle and mom were always going down the street to other bars to party, so I was left to tend bar, which I loved to do. I loved to stay busy and had a lot of energy. I had to use it for something, and this was a good cause.

It was fun meeting people who thought I was as grown up as they were. They thought I was old enough to be in the bar serving them, and I certainly wasn't going to tell them different. I actually enjoyed it—I had a lot of fun.

My uncle had one downfall: he liked to drink hard liquor. He would bring a bottle with him to work and invite everybody out to the backyard to have some. This did not help support our business.

It got to be a natural thing for some of our customers—to bring their own bottle and take it outside the back door. By then I was smart enough to know this business would not work out, especially with everybody drinking their own liquor. Uncle Russ had started something we could not stop. He was just a nice country guy and didn't know much about business.

I tried to talk to him, but he wouldn't listen to me. I'm sure he thought I was too young to know anything about the business world. But a lot of it was common sense.

For example, my uncle would say, "Let's get someone else to work tonight and we'll go and meet more of our neighbors." We would put anybody behind the bar and take off.

My mom would say, "OK, Russ, if this is what you want to do, we'll go and do it."

It was the blind leading the blind!

Or they would put me behind the bar to work the whole night by myself. I would go down to The Pike and bring my friends back too. So they had a good time and would bring a lot of other friends each time. This brought in money, but we were lucky we didn't get busted. They were happy to spend their money at our bar, because they were only seventeen or eighteen years old, and it was the only place they could get away with drinking. We were lucky we didn't get closed down.

We lasted about eleven months before we lost the business.

Mom had to go back to her airplane factory job. Uncle Russ went back to his logging in Oregon. My brother went back home to my grandma in Torrance. And I went back to The Pike to try to get my old job back at the basketball game—and I did. It seemed like I was always going back to The Pike. It was in the cards for me; my destiny for sure.

The people who ran the basketball game had bought a shooting gallery, and I got to work there instead of the basketball game. They had four .22-caliber rifles and one pistol that was a

.22-caliber. They used real bullets. I would challenge the sailors to outshoot the others for a few dollars, and most of the time I would win some extra bucks. It was a lot of fun. I learned to love shooting and got pretty good at it. I worked at the shooting galley for the next two years. By now my husband had returned from overseas, and I had gotten a divorce. We just couldn't live together in peace. Then I got another boyfriend, and that wasn't working out either.

Life was still disappointing me when I broke up with yet another boyfriend. This time I had my own pills. I mixed them with alcohol and said goodbye to the world and the pain that went with living.

Some friends found me and called an ambulance, and again I went to the hospital. When I got there, they put tubes down my throat again and pumped my stomach. I remembered real fast how much that had hurt the first time.

When I came back to life and was able to talk, I said, "Hey, doctor, I really don't want to be here, so can I pay you all the money I have so you can finish me off? Please, doctor, please help me out."

Of course he said no, and that landed me in the nuthouse for thirty days. That wasn't fun. There were very crazy people in that nuthouse. Again, the lessons were adding up. After the doctors examined me, they said I had had a stress attack and I could go home.

I had a phony ID that said I was two years older than I was, so it was no problem for me to walk out of the hospital by myself.

When I got back to The Pike, I was a happy camper. Being left alone and not told when to get up or when to sleep or when to eat or when not to eat was the benefit of working and being back on my own. Life was peaceful again.

CHAPTER 11

Bought Two Concessions on The Pike at Eighteen Years Old

WHEN I TURNED eighteen, I bought my first concession booth: a dart balloon game. Then I bought my second balloon game a year later. It was a lot of work, but I needed something to do with my time, and I enjoyed working with the people.

Unfortunately, I paid more than anybody for these games. That's why they sold them to me. But it was good; I made more money then I ever dreamed I could.

I would open at nine a.m. and close at ten p.m. on weeknights. Weekends I closed at eleven p.m. or midnight. We worked long hours, and it was a very physical job. We were always moving. Most of the time it was seven days a week for me, either working behind the booth or being the owner of two concessions and taking care of needed business affairs.

I remember one nice, sunny day when everybody was bringing their TVs to work at The Pike so they could watch the first man land on the moon. It was amazing. It happened right in front of our eyes! That day, July 20, 1969, was when TV captured Neil Armstrong walking on the moon. To think President Nixon was watching at the same time on his own TV! It was a sight to see and something I will never forget.

Later a story about Armstrong said that when he was asked by journalists about his thoughts on that historical first manned voyage to the moon, he admitted he had not had much hope of both landing on the moon and returning back to Earth. He said the crew members had been profoundly ecstatic and actually surprised that they had managed to successfully accomplish the most daring venture of humankind: sending the first humans to walk on the moon.

You can do all things—and you can do all things with the Lord's help.

I can do all this through him who gives me strength.
—Phil. 4:13

After work, I would go to the cocktail bar on the next block and dance my heart away every night. I loved dancing as much as I liked breathing. It was a great way to relax and have fun. The bartender would come across the bar and sneak in a few dances with me. That's how Don and I got acquainted.

One night Don said, "Phyllis, would you like to go to breakfast with me after I get off of work?"

"Sounds like a good idea," I answered. We talked for hours at the coffee shop and found out we had a lot in common.

After that, you didn't see one of us without the other if we weren't working—and we were both workaholic. Don worked at his father's business during the day and the bar at night. I was always at The Pike.

We moved in together, and I got pregnant. After the baby was born, we finally got married. Don's father owned a school that taught people how to be a high-class bartender or a high-class cocktail waitress. It was a great school. It was a lot more work then anyone would have thought. My sister Raylene took some of his classes; she became a cocktail waitress and worked at the best places in town. She did quite well for herself.

I would follow Raylene around and get really good recipes at the restaurants where she worked, and then I would go home and

Bought Two Concessions on The Pike at Eighteen Years Old

cook the recipes for everyone. Sometimes I would hang out at the school during the day to be with Don. It was quite amusing to watch how the school operated.

When Don and I had our wonderful baby boy, Bradley, he was a gift from God. He changed my whole life. I became a responsible adult. I sold my motorcycle, settled down, and became a mom. I had to make sure I would be there for my baby and I knew I couldn't be riding a motorcycle. I couldn't afford any serious accidents when I had a child. I loved my motorcycle, but I had to consider how to make a good future for Bradley and me. Realizing I was responsible for another human being made a big difference in my life.

My mother, grandfather, sister, and brother came to work for me. It was the best thing that ever had happened to our family; we never had made that much money before. The Pike was full of fun and good energy. Everybody was having lots of fun winning prizes for their girlfriends or kids, so the energy was very up and happy. It was great to be around happy people all day long. What a blessing!

After four years of working in my balloon store, my mom met a nice guy. She would go to the local bar, which was at the end of The Pike, where she would visit with her friends. That's how she met Todd. He owned three concessions on The Pike for about twenty years. Todd had a balloon store, Knock the Bottle Over, and a basketball game. He also traveled for about six months with the traveling carnival every summer.

Todd said to my mother, "Ruth, I would like it if you'd go on the road with me. I'm crazy about you, and we could work side by side."

He told my mom it was a good opportunity and she would be amazed at how much money she could make.

"Phyllis, Todd asked me to be his girlfriend and go on the road with him," she said to me later. "I already told him yes." Todd was boyfriend number six.

My mom was a good worker and a good-looking woman. I told her, "He's getting the better part of the deal. Good luck."

I knew I was losing one of my best agents, and I hoped she'd be safe on the road. Mom had a lot of spirit. She never gave up

The Carnival Girl

on having a special relationship. I knew she wouldn't be working for me when she came back. I know that sounds selfish now, but those are the kinds of things you have to think about when you have your own business.

Good things were happening for my mom, and she was happy. I was glad for her. Todd was a good man. I thank God he was good to my mom—it was certainly her turn.

After the first summer, mom returned and had nothing but good things to say about traveling with the carnival. She told me, "Phyllis you should try it some day."

"No, thanks," I said. "I'm not going on the road. I have a child to think about, and things are good right here."

Raylene and I on The Pike in Long Beach, California. Raylene was 23, I was 21.

Then I broke up with Don, my baby's father. Things were not good. After one and a half years, we divorced. It was the second time I had gotten married, but it was the first time for love. Yet this was for the best. He was a great guy but drank too much, and that was OK with me until we had our baby boy. Things were supposed to change. Don still worked at the bar, and he had a bad habit of bringing the bar home with him. They would come to our house making noise and wake up our baby. I got tired of chasing everyone out of our home at 2:30 a.m. each night. I tried to let Don know it wasn't working and it needed to stop, but he didn't hear me.

"Don't tell me what to do. I will have my friends over any time I want," he said.

By then I could see we were not on the same page anymore. It was up to me to turn the page and hope it would work out. I had to keep my sanity. After all, I was the one getting up in the middle of the night and in the morning with the baby. I was still working on The Pike and running two concessions, so I already had a lot on my plate. I needed my sleep and to have some kind of routine in my life, and I had to make sure my baby wasn't being awakened all hours of the night.

Somehow Don and I lost the happy medium in our life. We really loved each other, but were both going in different directions. It's a sad thing when you can't grow up with your mom and dad, as Bradley didn't, but sometimes it ends up that way.

CHAPTER 12

A New Life with Artie

I STARTED GOING to visit my mom at the restaurant and bar where she hung out, and I met Artie. He had a concession next to mine, but we never had visited before we met at the bar. He was one of the people who ran the office on The Pike. I never wanted to get to know anybody from the office. I tried hard not to get in trouble with them, but I did. My sweet grandfather would start opening up my balloon store before it was time, and he would start taking money. We had rules and orders from the office that nobody could open up before the other concessions opened. The Ferris wheel had to blink two times before we could open.

"Grandpa Jerry," I would say, "you make sure you don't take any money before the park opens."

He would answer, "No problem, Phyllis, I will wait."

But he never did. He was excited to be working and to be alive. It was cash money—he gave some to me and put some in his pocket. He was in his second childhood.

I also hated to go shopping with my grandfather. He always had to take something he didn't pay for from the store. Many times it was women's panties—when we left the store he would laugh about getting away with something and show them to me. I would tell him not to do that again, especially when I was with him, but again he paid no attention.

The Pike's office workers were strict, and I heard through the grapevine they were about to throw me off the midway. I didn't know what my family would do if that happened.

We gave Grandpa a little slack because he was old and I loved him very much. He had taken care of me for so much of my life, and now it was reversed. I couldn't fire him. I prayed they wouldn't catch him again, but of course they did. Luckily I had gotten acquainted with Artie, who was one of the bosses. After that I didn't get any more notices from the office about my grandpa, even though he was still opening up too early. People from the office would just come by and tell him to close until it was time to open.

After a while I started liking Artie. We enjoyed talking and kidding around with each other. The Pike bar was a handy place to go on a break or after work. Most everyone in The Pike bar was working on The Pike.

Then came the big question. "Would you like to go on the road this summer with me?" he asked.

I almost fell off my seat. The good thing was it meant he liked me, and I knew I liked him. I wondered where my life was going. It was about to change again.

"Artie, maybe another time," I said. "Things are going good for me and I have a son, so I need to stay here."

We kept meeting at the bar, having a few drinks, and enjoying each other's company. And then the question came up again.

"Artie, I can't go on the road," I replied. "Remember, I have a son. And he can't live in motels and hang out on the midway and not have a place to eat and rest and call his home."

"Phyllis, go and buy a little trailer," Artie suggested.

I thought about it—that sounded like a good idea. So I took some time to look into it and I found a motor home I liked. It would be a good solution, I figured, because my son could have a semi-normal life in his home on wheels.

I knew I would be giving up the best thing I had going for my son and me, so I was scared to make this move. The next day I met Artie in the bar.

"Artie, I have to sell my concessions before I can afford to go anywhere," I said. "I can't buy the motor home until I sell them. It's not going to work out until next year when I have more time to work on things."

"Phyllis, I already have a buyer for you and we can meet with him tomorrow morning," Artie said.

Come to find out, Artie and his partner wanted to buy the balloon store next to his restaurant. They had been planning to purchase it because they wanted to expand his restaurant and they needed the space.

So Artie and his partner bought both of my balloon stores and sold the one across from the Ferris wheel to someone else. Then they expanded their restaurant.

CHAPTER 13

Traveling with the Carnies

THIS IS WHEN the love bug hit. Oh, I was starting to go blind again, and you know that old saying ("love is blind"). Well, here we go again.

Artie was used to having things his way. He knew everybody and could put anything together. He didn't know what no meant. He could talk anybody into anything. He was the front man, the guy they sent in to put the deal together, the promoter, the patch man, and the man that made it work. He always got his way.

I didn't have a chance when he decided he wanted me to go. I was going, and that was how my life was going to be for the next ten years. Artie was totally in charge of my son and my life from then on.

So that's how Brad and I got on the road, traveling with the carnival and hanging out with Artie.

I was from a very poor lifestyle. After meeting Artie, life got exciting. Artie took me for my first shrimp cocktail and my very first nice dinner at an expensive restaurant. He took me to our yearly show-business dinner with ballroom dancing. We had all the fancy things—a motel suite that was out of this world, and matches and napkins with our names printed on them. Artie bought me diamonds and a fur of my very own. We had prime rib with all the trimmings and the evening finished off with a few cocktails and great memories.

Everything I learned working in the amusement business made the rest of my life easier and very successful in the business world in Long Beach, California. I had a good eleven years on The Pike. I also had a good six years of owning my own business on The Pike. I worked hard and made a lot of money.

The Pike had been very good to me. I would take my son to The Pike to spend the day with him, and my sister would bring her three children and they would have a ball. They got to ride the rides for free and eat whatever they wanted. They played whatever games they wanted for free.

There were a lot of benefits to working in an amusement park. My sister and I always lived next door to each other or down the street from each other. We were bringing up our children together like brothers and sisters. Things certainly turned around for me when I got into the amusement business.

The Pike healed a lot of what had happened in my past, but some of my biggest healing came through Artie. He taught me how to work, love, and trust again. He was the family I never had all in one. He taught me how to run a business and make it work. He taught me it was OK to party as long as you went to work every day (self-preservation). I was able to take what he taught me and use it the rest of my life in business, and I became very successful.

Artie was a great guy. I was very lucky to have him in my life.

My grandma had always been the one to take care of the family but it got shifted to me. I became the new healer in our family. Everybody came to me for all their money and personal problems and I tried to help them the best I could.

When I went on the road with the traveling carnival, most of my family went with me. They again worked for me on the road and made more money than a lot of doctors and attorneys made. They liked the traveling; something about it makes you feel free. The gypsy life was really appealing.

There was a lot of magic on the midway. Everybody loved it. We had many special days such as half-price or free for senior citizens, ten dollars for kids to ride all day, and free entry for handicapped people. We made sure people never left the lot without a nice prize in their hands.

It was fun to watch the men disassemble the giant rides and load them into their big trucks. They would back up to the rides and have the show on the ground within four hours and then load up the heavy rides and be ready to hit the road. It was organized and looked easy—but we knew it was a lot of work.

We were like everyone else, loving the freedom of the carny's life. One highlight of the carny's life is the romantic side. It was like the sailors who traveled all over the world and had a lover in every port. So did the carnies, and there were always lots of girls waiting for someone to take care of them and save them from their home lives.

Young boys who were underage wanted to join the carnival. They wanted to get away from home or run away from life. The carnival looked like an easy way to work and live. They thought there weren't a lot of rules on how you lived your personal life on the midway. Boy, would they have been surprised if they had joined us.

"Honey, there's a special thing about the carnival when the lights are on and the music is playing. You can hear the people screaming from the rides and having fun. It outdoes anything in Las Vegas," Artie would explain. "Close your eyes and imagine you're eight years old and you're seeing the carnival for the first time. You're smelling and hearing the new and exciting things. There is nothing better in this whole world than your very first carnival."

"Honey, you are so right," I said. "It's a thrill to think back to the first time I experienced a carnival. It looked good back then and still does now."

We had a lot of greenhorns wanting to try our business. They thought it was a piece of cake. But they found out how difficult it was! A few would try it here and there and most would only last one or two spots before calling it quits. They would book their game with the show, and of course they would be put way in the back, which was last call. Maybe the marks would have some money left by the time they got to their joint or maybe not—they still had to pay the same nut (rent) we did. But of course we got the people when they first came onto the midway.

I said, "Honey, they're not saying this is easy money anymore."

"I know, you are so right," Artie said. "They're probably saying there is no money in this business. They probably think we're crazy for being here and working so hard. Which is OK with us."

It was a secret to the outside world that we made so much money.

The lot man had everything to do with where you ended up on the midway—and a little grease always helped. Whoever greased his hands the most would get the best locs (location). The show owner had to know you and like you to get good locs. The lot man would go on the lot before anyone else and measure your space for you and put you name on a piece of wood. That's where you would be putting up your joint or joints. You had to be around a long time before you got any breaks in this business.

This business is not for everyone. You had to be willing to work hard and want the freedom that goes with the carny's life. You had to learn to take the good with the bad—there is no welfare on the road.

The '60s revolution was going on at the same time—free love, drugs, the Vietnam War, and equal rights for all. We saw lots of changes, lots of hippies, and they looked like they were having more fun then I was. They were hanging out at the beaches, going to the concerts, and they looked like they were eating and drinking well.

But this time I kept my senses about me and kept working and planning for the future for my son and me. Brad had been born September 12, 1965. I had to stay in bed seven and a half months during my pregnancy. I wanted him with all my heart—if I had moved around much I could have lost him. He was one of my best blessings and still is today.

When it was time to give birth, I was on The Pike checking on my two businesses. My water broke, so I called out to my favorite friends, two of the policeman whose beat was The Pike. I knew them well because they had worked on The Pike for the eight years I had been there. I yelled out, "Help, please take me to the hospital. It's time."

After I got to the hospital I was in labor for eighteen hours. Not what I expected.

When my son decided it was time to be born, he popped out at lightning speed. He was so fast, the doctor had to drop everything to catch him. I was happy to finally see Brad and to see he was perfectly formed. The nurses instantly took him away from me and put him in an incubator. They said he needed to completely develop his lungs but that he wouldn't be in the incubator long.

As soon as Brad was born, I forgot about the pain and discovered what real joy was. My heart was filled with more love than I ever knew possible.

Brad weighed only five pounds, and he lost a half-pound during the five days he was in the incubator. I had to feed him every two hours around the clock. I was so proud and excited to have created such a beautiful baby boy and to know he belonged to me. This was the best thing I had ever done, and I knew he would always come first in my life.

While I stayed in bed, my sister Raylene took care of my balloon concession games on The Pike. It was not something Raylene wanted to do—she didn't like being the boss and having all the responsibility—but she did it anyway. It was not an easy job, taking care of two concessions and being the boss to six people. They ran all over her, and she cried a lot because she was pregnant, which left her sensitive to everything. She had a hard time taking care of things, but she was a trouper and keep things going. That's what a good sister she was. I was blessed again. I'm sure I didn't appreciate her enough for all she did.

In 1968, when I left with Artie, I was twenty-six years old and my son was three. I was following my boyfriend on the road. He had a lot of concessions, and I trusted him completely. Whatever he said was OK with me.

Before we left The Pike, I had bought my motor home and packed it as full as I could get it. Artie took me out to the school grounds for lessons on how to drive it. I didn't think it was hard to drive, and I even got good at parking it between two cars. I whipped it around like it was nothing. Most of the time on the road, Artie drove one of the big trucks or his Cadillac, so I had to learn how to drive my motor home.

Artie was one of the owners and bosses, so I knew my son and I would be safe, and besides I was in love. I thought he was the best. I think I would have gone anywhere with him. He was the love of my life and still is to this day. Even though I'm not with him, sometimes I wish it could have been different from today. But we make our choices, and that's the way it is. We have to learn to live with things the way they are. I'm sure everything has turned out for the best, but sometimes I look back and wonder how it might have been.

CHAPTER 14

Bought My First Home

AFTER THREE YEARS on the road, I bought a cute little two-bedroom, one-bath home in Long Beach, California. It had a nice size yard that was completely fenced. I was twenty-nine, and my son was about five at this time, and we were happy to have our own home. The house made him feel so much more secure—you could see it in his eyes and the way he walked. There hadn't been enough room in the motor home for my son to move around, so we needed to settle down. He was ready to start school. This house was meant to be.

Let me tell you how it happened. I was definitely working with my angels.

I wanted to buy a house, so I went to town and found a real estate office and walked in. "I'm here to buy a house," I announced.

The real estate agent looked at me a little strange. This was when a woman didn't buy a house on her own. Women couldn't even get credit cards.

I was asked what kind of job I had, if I had been there at least two years, how much I made, and what kind of credit I had. I think she thought these questions were going to chase me away, but they didn't bother me a bit. I was there to buy a house and that is what I was going to do. I said I had no credit and I was a carny who traveled on the road eight months out of the year, which I had been doing for the last three years.

As I said all of that, she suddenly looked as though she was in complete shock and that I was crazy.

Then she asked me how much money I had for a down payment. I said I had eight hundred dollars.

She again looked at me like I was crazy. I had no idea what it took to purchase a house. I didn't know anything about the financing. I just knew I wanted to buy a home!

She stared at me and moved her head around a little. I could see her take a few swallows. She clearly didn't know what to say to me.

Then the phone rang. It was a single man still active in the military. He wanted to sell his house, and he would take eight hundred dollars cash for his equity. He was in a hurry because he had just been transferred.

The woman told the seller we would be right over. On the way to see the place, she told me I should buy it no matter how it looked since I didn't have to qualify for a loan to get it. The house was under a VA loan, which I could just assume once the owner cashed out his equity. If I didn't buy it right then, she said, somebody in her office would buy it. I was confused.

I had no idea what I was doing, so I asked my angels. They said yes, go for it, so I did right then and there. We wrote up the offer on the house and the seller signed and so did I. It was a done deal. I had made the biggest investment in my life! It was amazing how it went together perfectly.

God was always there looking out for my son and me. We were getting another blessing. In thirty days we were moving into the first home I had ever bought. I had saved the money and found and bought this house all by myself.

It was a fixer-upper, though. The first year, my son and I were on the roof patching it with hot tar, time after time. We had buckets all over. But we didn't care, we were happy with our new home. We took one step at a time doing repairs on that home, one after another.

CHAPTER 15

Back on the Road

WE WERE PROUD to be connected with the carnival and in show business. The carnival was much more than meets the eye of anyone living on the outside. People with the show had at least one or two animals that traveled with them. Everybody was an animal lover. I didn't have any animals, myself. I was allergic, which made traveling, life a lot easier.

We also had a monthly newsletter we could pick up at the cook shack any time. We caught up on what was happening with other shows and different people. The newsletter told us where things were happening and in which state and town. We had a yearly book that gave everybody information on what was going on and where the different shows and locations were in the U.S. for that year.

Most of us would meet at the cook shack at lunch or dinner with some of the other bosses and talk about the stories going on with the help. We were trying to keep order within the show, so we did a lot of reviewing of how things were going with everyone.

One morning we were talking about Robert and Sally. They were working in the dime-toss game. Rick said, "They have been getting drunk and haven't been able to do a good day's work for a while."

Artie said, "Rick, do you want me to take care of things?"

Rick said, "Sure would be nice. It's time they understood how things work around here. They really don't know the rules yet, because they are already asking other people for a job. They know they are about to get fired."

The help was not allowed to change jobs whenever they wanted. They had to get permission from the boss for whom they were working at the time. That kept everybody honest. We worked together on being honest with each other, especially with the help. We always knew what was going on from one game to another. The help had learned if they wanted to change jobs, they had to give their boss a two-week notice and then they could move on and were free to get a job with someone else on the show.

The newsletter gave us information about what shows were playing and where to get paperwork to offer a bid on those fairs each year. Sometimes after you made a bid on a show you wanted to play (and it was a good one), you would make a bid for two to five years. It was important to have a good reputation to get to play the fairs of your choice. You had to put down a good deposit to hold your bid.

Each winter we had a ballroom dinner and dance party. It was always in one of the best hotels in San Francisco or Los Angeles, and it was always formal dress. We even went to Palm Springs one year. The weather was great, and we ran into many movie stars because a lot of them wintered in Palm Spring.

Now back to working on the road. On a typical day, I would wake up in the motor home with my son, and we would take showers and get dressed to go to the cook shack for breakfast. I could smell the coffee calling me to get going. After breakfast I would put on an apron. When the call came for opening, I would go to work in a dart and balloon-store game. That was my specialty.

When I wasn't being the pick-up-money person every two hours from each agent in Artie's twenty joints, I would go over and pull up my awning and start blowing up my balloons to put on the backboard. There were two or three of us who worked in one booth so I had lots of help in the big spots we played. After all, we worked on commission and had to be there when it was busy. We had to make hay while we could and then close up for the evening and start over in the morning.

The weather was one of the most important things in our lives. It meant whether we were going to do well or not in each spot we played and how much money we were going to make—if any. We would try to figure out what the previous year had been like and how well we had done then. But it always turned out differently from year to year.

One of Artie's jobs was to go to the cook shack everyday to get info about other shows and the gossip of what was going on in our show for the day. That's how he and the other bosses could keep things running smoothly.

New people were coming and going all the time. They thought it was a piece of cake and found out it wasn't. A lot of carnies had habits like drinking and gambling. They always needed money. But that never stopped us from hiring them. We liked hungry people—it made them good workers.

We had our own light towers no matter where we went. The ride help usually stayed to themselves and the jointers stayed to themselves.

Artie would stay in the motel when my son was on the road with us. We were not married, so it wasn't proper to stay together in front of him. It was the way of the times. My son would stay with my sister while he was in school, which was about three months out of the year. The rest of the time he was always with me on the road.

Nowadays, a lot of couples have a baby first and then get married. Everything seems to change in time. If you wait long enough, everything will change whether you want it to or not. What you thought was a "do or die" rule, an idea, or the only way it could be, will change today or tomorrow. Who knows what tomorrow will bring? The only thing we could count on was change. The second thing you could count on was the same families would show up every year to work on the Foley and Burke Show.

When we went into a town, the people were waiting for us to show them a good time. They would wait in long lines. You could see the excitement in their eyes, especially the little children, when we opened the gates. How exciting it was to open the show each time! The people loved to see us come into town. Sometimes we were the only exciting thing that happened in their town for the whole year. Everybody loved the smell of the carnival with all the different aromas floating through the air and hearing all the carnival music. Now, when we played private parties, it was a lot different. There was a lot of booze and gaming going on, which was mostly played at night for adults only.

All the children that traveled with the fair were taught to go to work at the age of ten. The gypsy girls all loved Brad. They would follow him around all day long. That went on until we left the show, which was twelve years later. The gypsy families who traveled with our show were very nice families. They were just like us, trying to have a peaceful life and take care of their children. Most of them wintered in northern California, selling cars.

When Artie was staying in the motel, I just couldn't wait to see him at the cook shack every morning. It was like I was meeting him for the first time. The excitement was always still there.

Artie would say he really missed me and ask, "Is there anyway we can slip out tonight for a nice dinner and a little private time?"

I would get butterflies in my stomach and answer, "Yes, honey, I will try to get away."

I really couldn't wait to be in his arms again. But sometimes I wanted him to chase me again, so I had to play hard to get. It kept things interesting. We really enjoyed each other's company and liked hanging around together. It was real love! I was so much in love, I believed the world would come to an end if I couldn't see Artie every morning to get my kiss and hug. I lived and breathed Artie, and I wanted to make him happy.

Artie and my son were my life. Artie was my love, my protector, and they were both everything I needed in my life.

One morning Artie said, "I have some news this morning. I'm going to have to leave for a few days, and I will be back Friday. Phyllis, I have some business to take care of, but it won't take me long this time. When I get back, honey, we will have a nice dinner with Brad and then get a babysitter for a little while. Does that sound good to you?"

I said I would think about it and let him know when he got back. We were both so much in love I never had to worry about another woman. We thought alike, worked together, and loved to dance, sing, and party together.

The good news was no drugs were allowed on our show, and if they were found on anybody, those people would get beat up and kicked off the show. We were a family show, and we meant to keep it that way.

When you first came on the show at most fairgrounds, you would see the independent side, and then you would see the carnival side. One time I was walking through the gate at the Modesto Fair, and I could see a guy playing his banjo to the right, and I could hear the carnival music playing to the left. Each fair always had well-known stars who would sing and dance. A nice local singing and dance group would come one night of the week, and everybody would dance. We had a lot of country singers up on those stages, which drew a lot of people to the fair.

Some of the big names that played the fair circuit were Willie Nelson, Dolly Parton, Johnny Cash, June Carter Cash, Waylon Jennings, the Statler Brothers, Alabama, and many others. They all knew to come over to the office and get their free ride tickets. I enjoyed slipping away from my concession long enough to go over and watch the entertainers. It certainly helped to bring more people, and the carnival side always did well from the action.

When you arrived at the fair, the first things you normally would see were the wild hats, flying airplanes on a stick, fancy wind stars, yoyos, fans, plastic swords, sun hats, and much more. The independent parts of the fairs were fun to explore. They always had the latest flower assortment, new diet drinks, and new beautiful driftwood art to check out. They also had painting, handy-dandy kitchen accessories, new blenders, the latest TVs, stereos, the newest phone on the market, and much more.

The 4H clubs brought their great animals for us to see and watch in their competition for the blue ribbons. And the action was fun

The Carnival Girl

to watch. If I had been home, I would have bought one of those animals. They looked like they were fed well, and I'm sure that was some good meat. Then there were the beautiful racehorses to see and bet on. They were the main attraction at every fair we played.

We had three classes of people on the show, just as you would find in any town in America—owners, bosses, and workers. We had a lot of families who traveled with the show every year. And then we had the roustabouts, freeloaders, and of course the gophers.

There were plenty of rules, and they were not to be broken or you might find yourself out of a job with no place to live. They were for the good of all, and excuses were never good enough. You did it right, or you didn't do it at all.

You would have thought we were being run by some military or mafia the way we stayed in line. The family touch was very powerful. Most of the carnies came from broken homes or were orphans, so this was their home, which made us a loving and tight family.

Artie had about two hundred men at his beck and call any time he wanted them for anything. It was organized. That's why things went smoothly.

After we played about six little fairs, it was time to go to our regular show where we belonged each year. We played all the big shows. The biggest and the best show on the West Coast was "The Foley and Burke Shows," where we would get to see Russ and Ruth and enjoy their good food in our favorite cook shack. They only played with the Foley and Burke Shows from May to October.

It was nice to see Russ and Ruth. They had been running the cook shack for ten years. One year they arrived with a brand new cook shack trailer. They felt right uptown! There were new slots and holes on the rollout and the new set-up table was great, which made their job easier and cut their set-up time in half. We always had a good spread of food. I never had to worry about Brad having good food available.

The cook shack, which was mostly just for the carnies, had everything you needed. Brad especially liked his ham and bacon with two eggs and wheat toast for breakfast. We had hash browns, all kinds of eggs, bacon, ham, sausage, and baskets with different kinds of breads, jam, and fruit. When we were eating in the cook shack, we knew we would be getting something good to eat. There was also Russ's famous French toast and pancakes and his homemade syrup and jelly.

There was also food available on the independent lot, which had many different kinds of food to choose from. There were many brightly colored snow cones and every kind of drink, such as lemonade, Coke, Pepsi, root beer, strawberry soda, and much more.

The tables were covered with red and green tablecloths for the owners and bosses, who sat on one side of the cook shack. The silverware, salt and pepper shakers, and sugar were on the tables. The rest of the crew ate on the other side of the tent and got their own silverware, sugar, and salt and pepper. It was always a nice place to say good morning to everyone. Everybody was lighting their cigarettes, chewing their tobacco, and having their first cup of coffee as they awakened for a new day in show business. We wouldn't see each other for most of the day after that, if at all.

It was certainly a good feeling to be back home again. This was definitely the first place I could call home for a long time. So now I had two homes—one on the road and my second home with my son in Long Beach.

Russ always gave me a big hug and said it was good to see me again. "Phyllis," he asked once, "what about that son of yours? Is he here to keep the little gypsy girls in line?"

"Russ, you know me," I said with a smile. "I wouldn't have left town without him. Of course he is here." We always enjoyed seeing all of our friends on the Foley and Burke show, but we'd miss them in the winter. They were part of our family with our little town on wheels.

Everybody loved Brad. He had a nice personality and was a lot of fun to be around.

We had four different gypsy families on our show. They were not who you would see reading your fortune or looking into the future. I used to tell their fortunes for them from the astrology books I read. We always had a big laugh, and they wanted to know more.

The gypsies belonged to the same tribe but lived in different places in the winter. They had nice homes, and their boys went to school to get an education. There was no need for the girls to get an education because they went wherever their men went. I'm sure that has changed—we are talking fifty years ago. They still picked each girl's husband for her, which was very old fashioned. Even in those times!

Gypsies controlled the girls with fear. The girls would tell me nobody would take care of them except their own kind. They would never leave the tribe. If one of the girls did, the others would make an example out of them and did not take them back into the tribe. This scared them enough to go ahead and marry within other close tribes in their areas.

Gypsies had a lot of money, but they worked hard to get it like the rest of us carnies did. Their children worked side by side with them as soon as they were ten years old. They all kept to themselves and stayed out of trouble. They had an average of four or five of their own concessions, and they worked them. That way they got to keep all the money coming into the concession.

These joints cost them from fifty-thousand up to two-hundred-thousand dollars to purchase. One of their special games was the water balloon game where you shoot a play gun and pop the balloon. This game came put together in a traveling trailer—I would say it was one of the most expensive trailers on the lot.

They also had the horse race games that came with their own trailers and cost a bundle.

Gypsy children were taught to save their money for when they would get married and have a family of their own. In the winter, the gypsies had homes in Portland, Oregon, and Red Bluff and Redding, California.

Sometimes people would add some of their own games at events if we were playing a private party such as a Catholic Church festival or another organization. The liquor would come out, and they would have a big set-up with their own bar. There were gaming tables like roulette and cards, or even rolling the dice in their own pit game.

CHAPTER 16

Back to Coeur d'Alene, Idaho

THE PHONE RINGS, and I'm back in 2010, living in Coeur d'Alene, Idaho. It was my good friend Bobbie calling me back. I had called her to see if she was going to exercise class. I go Mondays and Wednesdays with a group of people called the Striders. Steve started the Striders with the intent to help seniors stay young and healthy by walking and doing stretches on a daily basis.

We walk every day at the mall and do an exercise class twice a week. It's a lot of fun, and we are always meeting new people. I've made a lot of new friends there. Steve traveled a lot in the United States and abroad. He had a band, and met a lot of people. During his travels, Steve saw people in other countries had to do a lot more exercise then we do in the U.S. He thought that was making them healthier than us, so he decided to start something that would help the aging to age well. Five years later we now have about two hundred Striders between Spokane, Washington, and Coeur d'Alene, Idaho.

The Striders are a group of fifty- to ninety-year-olds working to stay healthy and young It's a fun way to exercise and visit with friends. We have awards breakfasts three or four times a year where we win tickets to eat at local restaurants. It gets us out, even in the winter.

The Carnival Girl

The Striders are people from all walks of life. When you're a "certain age," where you come from doesn't matter. You are where you are at the moment.

While I was walking at the mall, I had the opportunity to meet people from the Eagles and the Elks clubs. There are all types of people in these clubs—some retired police officers from Los Angeles, firefighters, retired military, some construction business owner and operators, former real estate brokers and agents. Let's not forget the housewives and secretaries. People join the Elks and Eagles from all over. We have a lot of activities to raise money for different charities. There are mostly retired people in both clubs. There is a lot of fun going on in these clubs. If you get a chance, you should join them.

Winter in Coeur d'Alene is cold and snowy, so I decided to go south for part of one year. A lot of people go south for the entire winter, but I just went for thirty days. I picked a place called Optima Health Institute in sunny San Diego, California, that uses holistic life changes to heal and rejuvenate people. Winter is the perfect time to go when the weather is about sixty-five to seventy-five degrees.

Optima Health Institute is a place for people who work for movie stars—and people like me. The movie stars go where it costs almost six thousand dollars a month or more! I heard that the stars detoxify there at least once or twice a year to keep themselves healthy and thin.

I had a great time learning a new food plan, such as eating raw veggies, grass, and drinking different healthy drink potions. (At least that's what they said they were!) The drinks didn't taste good, but they were used as detox for poisons in your body. Others called it a "tune-up" for your body. Everybody I met while I was there said they return every year.

What a treat if you could afford it! By the time I went home thirty days later, I felt like a million bucks and had lost twenty-five pounds. And it was a lot of fun—we had different activities going on all the time to keep it interesting. I would call that a win-win, wouldn't you?

Back to Coeur d'Alene, Idaho

I just love going to my water aerobics class three days a week with an age group that is sixty-five to ninety-five years old. In the mall I also meet and walk with a group of women who are age seventy and above. After our walk, we sit around and visit while we have our morning coffee.

It's a delightful group. I really enjoy them. They will show you how good life could be if you work at staying healthy physically and mentally. We also pick a different restaurant each month to attend for our monthly luncheon. I love it. It takes me back to how people were in the old days—warm and friendly.

Now it's five p.m. and I'm getting ready to go the Elks for my weekly dinner and to say hello to another delightful group. Tonight it's steak dinner for ten dollars. I'll bring my three friends with me: Josie, Susan, and Sally. We'll have a great time.

The Eagles have good music on Saturday nights, and there are usually about six friends that all go together. Coeur d'Alene has lots of retired people and lots to do.

One Tuesday night when I went to the Elks on hamburger night, I was standing in line when I had the surprise of my life. I ran into my good friends Jack and Barbara. I hadn't seen them for about twenty-five years. I was in line when Jack walked up and said, "Excuse me, miss, is your name Phyllis Horne?"

Jack hardly had gotten the words out of his month when I turned around and screamed, "Oh, my gosh! It's Jack and Barbara from Sacramento, California. It certainly makes me think about my time in the carnival again and my time in the real estate business."

When I left the carnival in 1979, I had gone to work for Jack at Century 21 real estate in Sacramento, California.

CHAPTER 17

Entering the World of Real Estate

I HAD A real estate business in Sacramento from 1979 to 1991. If you haven't allowed life to beat you up as my mother did—bless her heart—you need to keep your faith and dreams alive.

Life begins at forty. By then you know how to survive in this world. You know what you like and what you don't like. You know what you are willing to do or not do for at least the next ten years of your life. You can pick something you are interested in for work or play and go for it.

I picked real estate, and it was the best thing I'd every done for myself. I had read a few books about real estate investments, and it sounded like the thing to do. I didn't have any money for investments, so I read about another way: credit cards! I took a shot. I knew I would have to buy and sell fast enough to make sure I didn't pay much interest.

There was definitely a technique to the credit-card game, and you had to learn it right away, or you would indeed end up paying a lot of interest. The market was moving fast at that time. I knew if I kept it going, I could get way ahead of the game and do well.

I definitely had to keep my nose to the grindstone. It was a lot fun and hard work. The rewards were good. I made a lot of money. Century 21 Real Estate was the first real estate office where I had worked, and it was one of the best. Everyone was like family. We worked together and tried to help each other. Of course, Jack and Barbara made it work like a family. They were a big part of my new life in Sacramento, and I always felt close to them. They were there with me when I was starting my new adventure in the real estate business. It was a team effort.

Jack was a retired First Sergeant from the Air Force. He worked and trained us hard, but I didn't mind. I had no complaints. We turned out to be the best agents in town. Jack and Barbara were always there if you needed them.

I also had a good friend, Alberta, who ended up opening her own office. She ran her business like a family also. I enjoyed working in her office with her. She ran a very friendly and fun office. We always had a good time—it was more like play than work. She started it with a friend, who was her business partner, for about ten years. They first started out selling and listing houses. Then they moved to working and managing different subdivisions. After that they became big landowners. Then they started developing the land, building subdivisions, building homes, and selling them. It took a long time to put that together, but it was worth it. They made a lot of money, but they worked hard to get very successful.

Later, they started buying commercial buildings and fixing them to sell or rent. I had the pleasure of working in their office, and I learned a lot from listening and watching. If business was slow, they would share other opportunities with me, giving me jobs at their subdivisions. Alberta turned out to be my best friend and still is today.

Alberta had worked with residential houses for about twenty years, so she was well prepared for everything in the business. I had only been in the real estate business for a few years, but I was always ready to learn something new. I would hear Alberta and her partner talk about trying something different, such as buying land and becoming builders, and I would say that sounds like something I would like to do also. Then I would just go and do it. I wasn't their partner—I was an agent in their office. But I trusted their judgment completely.

Entering the World of Real Estate

I really wanted to try different business adventures. I had nothing to lose, and I was still living from paycheck to paycheck. I bought some land with a small, old house on it. I then decided to split it into two parcels. I built a new home on one parcel. It was a lot more work than I thought it would be, because there were so many details. I had to pick out every color, size, all the different items and materials, and then I had to tell the builders where I wanted everything to go. I can see why people get divorced when they're building a house together. Lots of fun, but very mind-boggling.

Next, I bought a cocktail bar and the real estate with it in Rio Linda, California, near Sacramento. Everything was a new adventure to me. I was having lots of fun.

The last two years of my real estate career, I bought and sold for myself. I bought fixer-uppers, land, new homes, and commercial property. I thought they all sounded like fun things to do—and they were. The reason I did real well in the real estate business was I had no fear of trying something new time after time.

Peggy is another friend I met in the real estate business. One day we were having cocktails at happy hour at our local pub when Peggy told Alberta and me that she had a guy living in her house and she needed him to leave, but he wouldn't. Peggy didn't know what to do and asked our opinion. I hadn't been away from the carnival long, so I was still used to thinking in my old way, which was to handle things myself. I told Peggy I would ask my son to help her out. She asked what he could do, and I said he would remove the man from her house.

"Phyllis, if he could do that I would really appreciate it," she said.

I went home and talked with my son. I asked if he could do something to help Peggy. Brad replied, "It sounds like we have a job to do. Mom, we can handle this. He had grown up knowing if everyone stuck together, they could handle anything that came their way.

The next day we called Peggy and asked her if she was ready. Peggy said, "Phyllis, I'd never been more ready. Come on over. The timing is great."

Brad and I went over with five of his friends carrying baseball bats. They stood outside Peggy's house and called out loudly, "Tom, you have five minutes to give Peggy back her key and leave the house."

They said it again and told him it was his last warning. As their bats were going from one hand to another, Tom appeared in the window. He clearly could see they meant business.

Peggy was inside the house next to Tom, looking out the window. You could almost read her lips. She was nodding her head and pointing her finger at the boys.

Tom left peacefully. He wasn't about to tackle five young bucks.

On his way out, Tom asked Brad if he really would have come into the house and thrown him out. Brad said, "You only had five minutes, so you did good, Tom. Yes, I would have come in and taken care of business. I did have permission from Peggy, and I would have thrown you out. You wouldn't be standing there in one piece."

Brad added, "I like it when things go peacefully—but I'm prepared if they don't."

CHAPTER 18

Impressions of the Carnival

ANOTHER GOOD FRIEND I hung out with was Gloria. We had met when I had worked with Jack and Barbara. One day I was telling her how Artie, my ex-boyfriend from the carnival, wanted me to come and work a show with him. He was short of help and he really needed me. I told her I was going back to the fair to play one spot near Los Angeles—the Pomona Fair. I would do it to help Artie, but I could also pick up some big money in a short amount of time.

Gloria asked me to take her with me. I told her it was a lot of work and long hours. She said she had always wanted to work at a fair, so I said OK, and away we went to Los Angeles. It was going to be a long one—a full three weeks of sixteen to eighteen hours a day. Gloria said she could work hard and do the long hours.

We arrived in Los Angeles one day before the show opened, so we helped them set up for opening day. The ride jocks, ticket sellers, office crew, and everyone who worked directly for the show were there. When we got there, they were standing in line to get a draw from the last spot they had worked. Within two days they would get their complete paycheck from the last spot.

There was always a lot of preparation, and the show needed lots of manpower. They would be in a heap of trouble if they didn't have anyone to help them put the rides up and down in the air. The ticket booths had to be put up and down. Everything needed to be lined up for the show before opening. Then there was driving the trucks from spot to spot and getting the equipment ready. Actually, in the carnival business you are always working on getting ready to go to the next spot.

You don't want to be anywhere close to the cook shack after the carnival crew gets their draws. They start lining up to in droves to get some grub, and the cook shack is packed full.

Artie said, "Phyllis, we have to go real early in the morning to have our breakfast before the crowd gets there. Let's be smart about what time we go to dinner these next two days—we want to avoid the ride help and ticket sellers. We need to go about seven p.m. for our dinner, so try not to be late. Take off work about 6:30 p.m. and I'll meet you there."

"OK, Artie," I said. "I'll be there at seven p.m. and I'll bring my friend Gloria for dinner. I can get Susie to take my place for an hour or two."

Artie, Gloria, and I arrived early the next morning for breakfast. It was the only time our friends Russ and Ruth could have a little breakfast or some coffee with us. They were too busy the rest of the day. We always made some time for them and we really enjoyed their company.

Soon the three weeks were up, and Gloria was ready to be done.

When we got back from working on the road, Gloria said, "Oh my, I had no idea it was this hard." She was glad to be back in her world and done with that.

This is what Gloria said about the carnival in an essay called "Neighborhood" that she wrote for her master's degree in business:

> The neighborhood I shall describe is an unusual one indeed. It is not stationary nor on a particular street. This vibrant neighborhood is known to almost everyone as a carnival. About three weeks ago, I had the opportunity to live with and work at the carnival. A dear friend of mine, who is now a successful real estate agent, once owned part of a carnival.

Impressions of the Carnival

Her mother usually looked after things for her, but due to ill health was unable to travel to the Los Angeles fair. So my friend and I took three weeks off work and flew to Los Angeles to work the carnival. In this period of time I learned to identify with the carnival, benefactors, and occupants, which are known as "carnies." Actually a carnival does have a main street, which is typical only to carnivals, and is simply known as the midway. About six a.m. the doors begin to swing open on the various camp trailers, beds under the rides, beds on the ground, motor homes, tractor trailers, beat-up old Chevys, and whatever else the carnies can find to sleep in.

The carnival and the midway are slowly coming alive. You will even spot some carnies climbing out from under trucks, buses, or even in some cases makeshift carnival booths, as this proved to be the best accommodations for the evening. By seven a.m. you can smell the aroma of bacon, sausage, ham, and eggs. Then the strong brewing coffee was calling our name. These breakfast smells combine in the air with cigar smoke as the cigar smokers are rising and breakfast is being prepared. Breakfast is being prepared in a portable building on the midway known as the cook shack. Actually it is a cafeteria on wheels, which caters mostly to the members and workers of the carnival and not often to the patrons. At precisely 7:30 a.m., the lines for breakfast are long and filled with an amazing assortment of human beings.

I finally meet Artie, who was my friend's boyfriend for years. And he certainly was not dirty or tacky. He spent his nights in the finest motor home money could buy. His clothes were always freshly laundered. I recall razor sharp creases in his immaculate black slacks, shiny well-polished shoes, and a shirt of bright red silk, which I was sure was expensive. On his pinky finger was a huge diamond ring that always glistened in the early morning sunlight as he puffed on his two-dollar cigars.

There was no dinner or lunch rush, as these meals were eaten during the day whenever business slacked off long enough to grab a bite to eat. After breakfast is over, the real beehive of activity begins. Carnival booths must have the canvas coverings raised, and the vacant holes where stuffed animals stood the night before replenished.

The shelves must be filled with teddy bears for the next lucky winner, who will spend twenty bucks trying to win a teddy bear worth $2.98. The jointers in the balloon and dart booths are busily blowing up balloons to replace the ones that had popped the night before, or had merely deflated during the course of the night.

The popcorn wagon is popping fresh corn. The ice machine is grinding away in preparation for the influx of children buying strawberry red, lime green, bubblegum blue, and other assortments of flavored ice cones throughout the hot day. The ride jocks are busily tightening whatever bolts have loosened up, and greasing the Ferris wheel, Tilt-a-Whirls, octopuses, and assortment of wild rides. They must keep running nonstop so the money flow is continual.

Finally, ten a.m. arrives, the carnival gates are open, and the fun-seekers pour in. The pace never lets up from sunup to one a.m. when the big wheel (double Ferris wheel) flashes on and off twice, signaling the workers the day had finally come to an end.

You'll find the fat lady standing next to the world's thinnest man, followed by a person who is known at the carnival as a "ride jock." He has his sleeves cut off and looks as though he slept in his clothes all night, which I can assure you is exactly what he did. His blue jeans look as though they have never met up with a washing machine or laundry soap since they first graced his body. Many of the ride jocks sport a gold or silver earring in one ear.

Like most everyone else who has strolled down the midway, I thought of these characters as being the average residents of the carnival, but I found out differently. The carnival residents are made up of many human components—some rich, some poor, some immaculate, and some look as though they have never bathed. The ride jocks are usually hired help who lead a life without purpose and follow the carnival to support their bad habits, such as booze, drugs, or whatever else it may be.

Impressions of the Carnival

Their bosses are usually intelligent, relatively well-fixed men and women with good personal hygiene. These people are known as the operators and are not usually in the public eye. The term "operators" is derived from the fact that these people are the owners of the rides and the game booths.

Game booths are known as joints, and the people who work them are called the "jointers." The entire human makeup of the carnival is referred to as these three: jointers, ride jocks, or operators.

The operators can be seen collecting cash from the jointers or ride jocks at regular intervals and basically remain in the background counting their cash. One operator, who struck me as particularly colorful, was a big, strapping Italian man known as Artie. He had black curly hair, stood about six feet tall, and believe me, when he said, "Jump" his help said, "How high?" On a typical day you will find him strolling down the midway with a brown canvas bag collecting money from his jointers, as he chews on a large greenish Cuban cigar.

The ritual of dropping the canvas coverings over the now half-empty prize booths and shutting down the motors on the rides begins. By the time this feat is accomplished, it is two a.m.

The weary carnies find refuge for the remainder of the night in whatever sanctuary their status offers, only to get up and begin again at about six a.m. As a child I dreamed of the glamorous life of a carny—what a joke. I have never known of any people who work so hard day and night, day in and day out, nonstop for their money.

The three weeks I spent there will remain indelibly stamped in my brain as one of the most eye-awakening experiences I have ever had. While we stand on the outside thinking all carnies are dirty characters, some are driving their shiny new Cadillacs to town in the evenings and eating the finest steaks in the finest restaurants the town has to offer. It really wouldn't be such a bad life if you were one of the operators and wanted to spend your life traveling. The carnies' favorite song is Willie Nelson's "On the Road Again"!

The Carnival Girl

Well, there you have it from the mouth of a writer getting her master's degree in business. Gloria and I think we've both seen a lot of things alike in the carnival business. By the way, she got an A+ on her essay. They loved her story.

This is what my sister Raylene had to say about the carnival and her traveling days:

> There are a few things that stand out in my mind about my "carnival days." Some are happy and funny, and some are a little scary. The most pleasant memories are the ones where the kids would bust a balloon and win a prize.
>
> Most of the time, unknown to the boss (which was my sister, Phyllis, or Artie), even when they didn't bust a balloon I'd give them a little prize anyway. Their little smiles or laughter were my rewards for doing my one good deed for the day. This went on over and over again.
>
> People don't realize the carnival business isn't "all" about the money. It's about being one big family. Proof of that came to me when a very large, mean-looking man jerked one of the big teddy bears off of my stand and took off running with it.
>
> I yelled, "Hey you! You can't do that!"
>
> He ignored me so I decided to test something I had heard about. I yelled, "Hey, Rube!"
>
> I had really hollered the words loud, and to my amazement the other people who worked in the stands jumped out (some with baseball bats). The carnies then surrounded this guy. He handed the bear back to one of the guys nearby and took off, which started out as a fast walk and then turned into a fast run.
>
> That's how we looked out for each other, like a family would.
>
> It has been about fifty years ago, so I don't know how the carnival is today. Hopefully, the new carnival people can walk away with

some fond memories as I have. We always had a good time tearing down the show, getting ready to move on.

There were a lot of great parties on the midway. After the big shows we were treated with all the great food you could ever eat and all the free booze you could ever want. After removing the bumper cars, we used the floor under them for some great dancing. It was a great experience, and I'm sure glad I got to be on the road with the carnies even though it was only for a short time in my life.

It was a great learning experience for me about people.

Thanks for listening,
Raylene Horne

This is my now-deceased mother's comments about her time traveling on the show with the carnies:

The hours are sure long. It is one of the most physical jobs I've ever had. It is one of the most traveling jobs I've ever had. But I've never had so much fun in my life on any other job. I absolutely love it, and I'm making more, lots more, money then I've ever made. You get to work outside and have fun with the customers all day long, and you get paid for it. How good is that! I got to hang out with my family all day. I loved that part more then you could imagine. All and all, it was one of the best times of my life. I traveled for about five years, and then the hours got to be too much for me, seeing I was getting up in age, but I will tell you I sure do miss being on the road with my blood family and the rest of my family.

If my mother was here, she would say thanks for all the good times on the road; God bless you. God bless her—we sure love and miss her!

Grandpa Jerry said he loved the carnival and wanted to do nothing else but work there. He used to say the kids were more fun than a barrel of monkeys. He was retired, so he had all the time in the world to enjoy the traveling. My grandma had already died, so he was lonesome and bored without the carnival. My grandpa could still work those long hours, day after day. He was a hard worker and a strong man. I loved him and I miss him.

Brad, my son, says the carnies were like his family. He says he misses that great feeling of having so much family around also. He told me for the longest time he kept looking to fill the void. Brad said he was not able to do so. He couldn't find that big family feeling again that he so loved. Then he decided to create his own. Now indeed he has his own family. He had five children and now has seven grandchildren.

Brad said he loved the road and all the traveling that went with it. He loved knowing Artie and would love to see him again. He also said he has a lot of good memories from his childhood.

He was the youngest of our family on the road. Actually, part of his young life was on the midway from three to fourteen years old. So I'm going to say he had the most fun of all. He got to ride all the rides free. He also played all the games free. He always had all the carny kids to play with. He started working at age ten. He would work for a different family and I would hire their kids to work for me. Brad says he learned about people and how to communicate well from the carnival.

Not too many people can fool Brad; he was a student of people his entire childhood. Today he now enjoys and loves being with his family.

Michael, my nephew (Raylene's son), says:

> During the time I spent on the road, I truly enjoyed all of it. The traveling on the show with the carnies, working in the joints, and meeting all the different people was great. I also made a lot of money. I would work side-by-side with the adults, and I was paid the same amount, which was a great feeling.

One of my best memories was knowing Artie, and I would like to see him again someday. I rode the rides and played the games for free. That was pretty cool. I loved the traveling and the people. I had lots of fun. I'm glad I had the chance to work with the carnies at one time in my life.

I'm fifty years old today, and I have lots of good memories, from all my time on the road. It was a great adventure.

Sincerely Michael

My brother, Ronnie, says he loved the carnival and would do it again if he were younger:

It was a free world and lots of action, which is just what I like. It was a lot of hard work, but the people that you traveled with were the best. The money was also good, and lots of girls were around all the time. Right up my alley.

How could you complain? Lots of good memories, Ronnie says.

All I can say is traveling on the road with the carnies was the best thing that ever happened to my family and me! Artie showed us a new life, and it was a good one. We all loved it and we could support our families. I'm so glad I got the chance to experience the carnival life.
It's a memory I'll hold close to my heart forever.
Phyllis

CHAPTER 19

Real Estate in Rio Linda, California

A LOT OF events happened in the real estate business. Jack and Barbara were there when I started on my new real estate business, so they shared an important time in my life. It was a big surprise for me to see them again at the Elks, and I never thought I would. I was happy we had lots of good old times to talk about. They brought me up to date on people we knew in Sacramento.

I loved the real estate business. It was good to me until 1982 when the market and economy fell apart. What a jolt that was! By then I had bought five houses and was ready to make a lot of money on my investments. Instead I had to give my real estate investments away to somebody who had a nine-to-five job and could take care of them and pay the negatives on the properties. They were the only people who were financially stable. They didn't have to qualify or have good jobs to assume the loans.

I wanted to save my credit because I had just built up great credit. I had negatives on each property, which meant I would have had to have come up with an extra four hundred dollars per month to keep them going—not the easiest thing for me to do in a down market. I figured I could start up again when the market turned around.

The Carnival Girl

I read a few books about the ups and down of real estate. It would be a good four to five years before things started picking up. In between I had become a property manager so I could survive. By this time I was following in my mother's footsteps in some ways, but instead of being an alcoholic I was a workaholic. That was certainly better on your health and your pocket! I married only twice—not like my mom marrying five times.

My boyfriend Ed and I had a trucking business together from 1982 to 1985. We had four trucks and two flatbeds. We hauled mostly lumber from Los Angeles to Oregon. I was still a Realtor, but business was very slow. You couldn't live off my real estate business alone, so it was the trucking business, firewood business, and the property management that kept us going and kept my plate very busy.

I had bought a big piece of commercial property. It was bare land, and I fenced it completely. We used this lot for the firewood business in Rio Linda, California, which was in the countryside about ten miles from downtown Sacramento.

We parked the motor home on the lot inside the fence and used it for an office. We sold a lot of firewood. It was a booming business. People were trying to save on their electric bills in a down market and economy.

It was close to the bar I had bought, which was one of the busiest bars in Rio Linda. I didn't want to operate a bar. I already knew what it entailed, and I didn't want any part of it. So it was sold right away for a small profit.

Rio Linda was a popular place for famous country singers. Okie Paul had a nightclub called Detour Inn in Rio Linda, about a quarter of a mile from my house. I think he might have even written the song "Detour Inn," I'm not sure. But he sure did know how to sing—Okie Paul had a great voice. I would go down to his nightclub and listen to him sing "Detour Inn." He'd also sing the song his wife, Olla Louise, wrote, "Mr. Fire Eyes." These were very popular songs at that time. It was also a popular place for Willie Nelson and Dolly Parton. They would come to our country town when they had a week or two in between shows. They were great.

I really enjoyed them. They would sneak into town hoping not to be noticed. They told us they were trying to get a little R and R before their next show. They would say they just couldn't stay away from singing, even for a little wile.

I was answering the phones one evening when I got a call from Okie Paul. He wanted to sell eighty-eight acres in Rio Linda. He really didn't know me from his nightclub, which was best if we were going to do business together. I kept it business and didn't say a word about his nightclub. I put his land on the market and ended up selling it to my best friend, Alberta, and her business partner. They were doing a lot of land developing. I disclosed that I knew them, but Okie Paul didn't care. He had his price, and that's all he cared about.

This was a big project. Alberta and her partner kept the land for about ten years. They had to do a lot of work and spent a lot of money on this property before they could make a profit. They decided to develop it and sell it to some builders they knew. They had to spend a lot of time in the planning department to get the zones changed, and they had to get a lot of permits to get it ready for the builders to make a subdivision out of it. Then they had to wait for the down market to go away and the good market to come back. Once it did, the property got split, and they started putting in the streets.

I was glad for the sale. It made me a lot of money. But Alberta and her partner made a mint. It was ten years later that they finely sold this property.

During this time I was with Ed, my last boyfriend. I said, "If we could live together for five years and still be happy with each other, we could get married." Needless to say, we lasted four and a half years, and it was over. I guess it really wasn't meant to be. We were fighting a lot, and I couldn't trust him anymore. He was saying one thing and doing another. I do believe you need five years to see all sides of a person. That's why you should wait before jumping into a marriage. Now this was another relationship down the drain.

Ed was drinking too much, and that's not how I wanted to live my life. I wanted to stick to the plan we made together and set ourselves up for our retirement. I had worked hard, and I wasn't going to let him blow it for me. It was getting close to the time when I wouldn't be able to do anything about my retirement, because I would be there, so I wasn't taking any chances. I really wanted it to work out, but there was no chance. I knew there wouldn't be anyone there for me, so I had to take care of myself. He talked about how he was celebrating the great success we were having in the trucking and firewood business. With my being in the real estate business, I guess we were doing well. But things really didn't pick up again until 1986—that's when I went back to real estate full time.

After I went back to working in the real estate business, Artie, the love of my life from the carnival, came back and asked me to move to Las Vegas with him. He was going to become the manager of Circus Circus in Las Vegas. I couldn't wait to go. I had really missed him very much. From the day we met, we were like one. We were always on the same page—except when he wanted something for himself, he could be a little selfish. I always had to watch out for that side of him.

I said yes. I still loved him and wanted to be with him. I would have given up my real estate career for him. Artie said we would have to finish the season out on the road first. I wasn't going back on the road. I knew I might not have enough money next time to leave. So I played it safe and said, "When you have a date that you will be going to Las Vegas is when I'll be leaving the real estate business."

But he couldn't give me a date. He said again "after we finish up with the season." I knew how good Artie was at talking anybody into anything. He completely ran my life for all the years we were together. He said he wanted to get married after we moved to Las Vegas, and that sounded good. Again I said yes. He never called me.

Artie never made it to Las Vegas. It was just a story to get me back on the road so I wouldn't or couldn't leave again. In the back of my mind, I was wishing it were true, so I let him break my heart again.

That's the way it is sometimes, and life does go on. Artie said, "Phyllis, you know I love you more then anyone, and you're the only women I have ever loved besides my mother."

Real Estate in Rio Linda, California

When Artie had a few drinks, he would tell everybody how much he loved me and that I was the only one for him. I didn't know he would be the only one for me for the rest of my life.

I never really loved anyone else like I did Artie, because no one could stand up to who he was to me. I wished it could have had a different ending.

So now I was ready to go back to the real estate investment business again, full force, and this time I figured I knew how it worked. I didn't want anything to do with old or new relationships. I had figured out it was easier to be a workaholic than to be in love. I needed to find serenity in my life, and some security sounded good to me. I was done with the relationship problems.

I worked extra hard and became successful. I loved every part of the real estate business.

I made sure this time when I bought my investments that they would pay for themselves. They would have to rent for the amount of the payment or more. There were not going to be any negatives on my properties. I bought eight new properties, and I watched the market going up, but I knew it wouldn't last for more then four years. From 1986 to 1990 I bought and sold eight houses.

When the market was moving at more than 10 percent each month, I knew it was time to get out and move on with my life. In the real estate business, timing was everything. If your timing was off, you could be the most brilliant person in the world and still lose everything. It was an eight- to ten-year cycle of ups and downs, so you had to be paying attention.

This was a big lesson in the real estate business. I had gotten the lesson the last time around, so I was ready this time to go for the gusto. It is definitely a gambling business on which you are betting to win. It takes a lot of guts, and you have to read about the history of real estate and do your homework. I was learning how to ride the waves of the real estate business. That's what we called the ups and downs in the investment world.

I loved servicing the different people and helping them find their dream home or their investment property. Alberta used to say, "Phyllis, you hear and say what you want to be trying next or what your new project is, and then you go and do it. You always have a success story at whatever you are trying. I have never met anybody like you. You have no fear about trying something new."

"Alberta," I said, "I never had anything in life, so what do I have to lose?"

Alberta was right, I had no fear, and that was the secret to my success. I never worried about how it was going to work out. I had faith my angels were there for me.

"Phyllis," Alberta said, "there was the time you heard us talking about buying some land and becoming developers. So then you went and bought some land and you became a land developer."

"Alberta," I said, "It was a lot of long hours and hard work, but I liked the challenge."

All I can say is wow, becoming a developer was more fun than anything. To see it come together was great. You buy the land, split the property, and create lots. The builders create houses, and the buyers come along, and they create a home for their family. It feels good to be part of process.

I had to ask Alberta for information on how to complete things, and she shared her experience with me. I always finished whatever I was working on at the time, no matter how hard things were. Alberta was my angel, always helping me out. There are many angels in this world. I always had mine with me wherever I went.

Alberta taught me how to:

1. Go to an engineer.
2. Have maps drawn.
3. Go to the planning commission.
4. Go to the city council
5. Get public reports.
6. Split the property into lots.

I named one street after my son, Bradley. That was a lot of fun. I would sell the lots to a builder, and they would build houses. Then I got paid, and I paid the seller the money I owed him. I bought on a lease option, which means a small down, and you finish paying at a later date.

This kind of project was challenging. I went away a happy camper. I didn't have to put up hardly any money up front to complete the deal. It took about six months to complete this deal, and I made a nice profit.

Then there was a five-acre property with a one-hundred-year-old house on it. I bought it. It had about a hundred years of junk on the property I had to remove. Brad offered to remove the junk. He did a great job. We were partners in a lot of different kinds of jobs like this one.

Brad was always looking for an extra job to make money for his family. Our work was cut out for us. It took all of Brad's friends and two years to remove every piece of junk. I paid them good money. Brad was my partner in most all of my adventures. We always worked side by side. Whatever we created, half was his.

The old house had its own great character. It had a giant living room—called a great room today—plus a giant kitchen and two small bedrooms. There were four big sheds Brad had to tear down later. But before we tore them down, we bought some chickens and pigs and had a few cows. That was an adventure all in itself.

I split the property and then built a new house for myself. It was a beautiful, country setting. I planted fifty additional trees, which gave it the finishing touch. Brad and his new wife and baby girl lived in the old house on the same property. The new house I built was a three-bedroom, two-bath, 1,600-square-foot home. I decided to be my own contractor, so I got the subcontractors lined up. It was my first time building my own house, and it took about five months to complete. I tried to have subs follow each other, one after another, but that didn't always work out. It seemed like we were always waiting for one or two of the subs at different times. They had to finish another job before they could come to work on my job, and sometimes that meant two weeks or even a month or so.

I don't think I would ever try that again unless I was going to make a nice profit. I think I would leave it to the builders. I didn't know what I was getting myself into. I can at least say I did it once. There is nothing like creating your own home where you're going to live. I did enjoy it when it was all done, though.

The Carnival Girl

Later, my son and his wife moved out of the old house and closer to town. I rented the old house out to a nice young couple, and that helped us with the payments. I enjoyed the house for about three years before we took off and moved to Oregon. My son had bought his own house within one year after I completed my home.

In 1979 there were four of us gals working the real estate market together and raising our children by ourselves. This was a real challenge for us. We worked in the same office at first, and then we split up and went to work in different offices.

We stayed in touch. We went to happy hour after work and shared the experiences of being single moms working on only commission. We were so busy that strange things happened, like someone putting the milk in the cabinet instead of the refrigerator. We talked about how at home we would put clean clothes back in the dirty clothes hamper after folding them and not being able to find them again in the morning.

We were all going on overload. We all had lots of funny stories from working in the real estate business, which was new to all of us. It was the new world of women working and making it on their own—being single moms—and we were some of the pioneer's.

We all were worried we might not make it in the real estate business. So we worked extra hard. All of us became very successful and had our pictures in the paper all the time. We were always the top producers in the Sacramento area.

When MADD, Mothers Against Drunk Drivers, was created in the Sacramento area, we knew everybody involved. We knew the gal who ran over the pedestrian jogging down the street, because she was our secretary. The one that got ran over was also a real estate agent in my office. We had been coming from a party and had a few drinks in us. It was a sad day for all of us.

The media decided to make this a good example to the whole world. Our dear friend, who was a nice and a caring person, went to prison for a long while. When she got out, I'm sure she was still feeling very sad. I'm sure her life was over forever as she knew it. I know she was wrong and needed to pay, but just because she made the wrong decision one time, her whole life changed forever. It was sad to see how it turned out.

The real estate office, the title company, and the mortgage company quit giving us parties to celebrate our success in the real estate market.

CHAPTER 20

Brad and Firewood

IT WAS TIME for another business adventure Brad and I could do together. He already had a pickup truck, so we went into the firewood business for three years.

At four or five a.m., a truck would drive onto our five-acre property with a twenty-foot flatbed trailer. It was filled with a lot of wood. It could hold twenty cords of wood. We had to get my son's friends to help us unload the truck, because we only had an hour.

I always got involved helping unload the truck. Then my son would load his pickup with one to two cords and get started with his day. He would deliver about five cords a day. He always outworked his friends. I would work the phones and book the appointments when I wasn't throwing firewood from truck to truck.

When I broke up with my boyfriend, he came over in the middle of the night and stole our wood. I called the police, and they made him give it back. Hurray again for the police! I loved it when things went the right way.

The second year we bought a dump truck, which made our life a lot easier. We could make more deliveries per day, about ten to twelve cord. Brad also had a lot less wood to throw. Brad was tough and was used to working, and he loved outside work. I was proud of his hard work and dedication. He worked and saved enough money for a down payment on his first house.

Brad was twenty-two years old when he bought his first house. I was twenty-eight when I bought my first house. I was proud he had a level head on him. Yes, I found him a good deal. He and his wife, a baby girl, Erica, who turned five years old, and Brian his baby boy, who was a little over one year old, were very happy to have their own home. They moved into a nice two-bedroom home. I forgot to mention he had his first child at seventeen years young. They lived with me for a while. I was glad to have them. We got along well. When I wasn't working, I got to be with my granddaughter and grandson. My son was always ahead of his time in life; he was very mature.

Then I got real sick—I was sleeping on the job.

I was still selling real estate when I started sleeping twenty-two hours a day. I would make an appointment with a client to show a house and meet them there. Then I would have to go around the corner to take a nap in my car before I could drive myself home. I couldn't stay awake long enough to drive home.

The doctors tried test after test and they couldn't find out what was wrong. Finally, they found out I had burned up my thyroid from stress. After they tried a dozen different medicines on me, we finally found the right thyroid pill. It worked for about seven years, and then they said they were not going to make that particular pill anymore.

"Phyllis, I'm sorry but the patent ran out, and they're not going to renew it," my doctor said.

"Doc, what am I going to do now?" I asked.

"There is nothing to replace it with. I'm sorry, Phyllis," he replied.

I went to a naturopathic doctor, and he took care of me. I asked how I was going to stay awake. He said he could make the medicine for me, thank God. I now take a natural thyroid pill, and everything has worked out well. I take nothing else to this day. I still order from him twenty years later.

Brad and Firewood

My son was also a trucker, and he worked for my boyfriend to help us out and to make his living. He was the best trucker my boyfriend ever had. Brad was on the ball, and my boyfriend made more money than he ever made. But when my boyfriend and I broke up, he wasn't nice to me, so he lost the best trucker he ever had. No more trucking job! But Brad and I were always OK with making a living. We had many different projects going on.

When my grandson Brian was old enough, my uncle would take Brad and Brian hunting and fishing in Oregon on the Indian reservation once a year. They would always bring us some good deer meat and trout.

Sacramento was the first time I stayed in one spot for long—not the same house but the same town. I was settling down a bit at thirty-nine years young. I actually made some long-term friends for the first time and still have them as friends today. We had moved around so much when I was a kid that I didn't get a chance to make any long-term friends.

I had family in Sacramento, which made it easier to settle down. My favorite Uncle Russ was there.

Brian said, "Grandma, I feel like I'm back in the days of living off the land. Hunting and fishing just to feed your family. It's like the cavemen lived."

I thought that was fun and exciting to hear. After all, he was such a youngster.

CHAPTER 21

Carnival in the '60s

BACK TO THE carnival again in the '60s. What a time it was. We were starting our road trip for the season. As we traveled down the road in our motor home, we sang our favorite song by Willie Nelson, "On the Road Again." We loved it. When you travel a lot, you feel free. We were like little children, living only for the moment.

Indio, near Palm Springs, is where we started each year. We went from March to late September or October, weather permitting. Artie was a good-looking, six-foot Italian with a nice personality and great body. I was a good-looking redhead, five-foot three inches and one hundred thirty pounds with lots of energy. Sometimes I was even a blonde.

Artie was very jealous, so everybody stayed away from me. They would only talk to me when Artie and I were together. They didn't want anybody to get the wrong idea. He was the boss, and they didn't want to make him mad and get fired. When Artie would leave town for a few days to take care of business, he would always have somebody watch over Brad and me. He wanted to make sure we were OK while he was gone. It was also a big control game.

I was only to know what Artie wanted me to know. Nobody else would ever tell me anything that was going on. I did feel isolated at times, but they knew about Artie's temper when it came to me. I loved Artie unconditionally, so I just went along with whatever.

Artie was a big gambler. We started out the same way every year: broke.

"Artie," I would ask, "is it time again?"

"Yes, Phyllis, bring out the pots and pans. It's time to start cooking."

I remember the brisk mornings as I was cooking to feed twenty people the beans and potatoes I had made. Everybody was pleased I was cooking again; they liked my cooking and were glad to get some grub in their stomach. I made breakfast, lunch, and dinner for the first ten days we were on the road. By then we would have some money coming in so everybody could start feeding themselves.

Every morning I walked out on the midway to get into my balloon store and start blowing up the balloons to fill the backboard. I would ask the two jointers on both sides of me for some help if I was alone, and they would. Tim had a ballgame on one side—knock the bottles over. Joe was on the other side with a machine-gun game.

We played the Indio show for five days and prayed for no rain. Sometimes we got rained out at the Indio fair. It was the end of February/first of March, which is a rough month for fairs. Sometimes we would only get rained out for one day. We always started out with a nice green lot and ended up with a muddy one. I was sure hoping it wouldn't rain too much. It might make it hard to get off the lot like it had in the past.

"Phyllis, honey," Artie said, "get ready. We're going to dinner with some of our friends from the show."

"OK, I can be ready in thirty minutes," I said.

I was so excited. It was the first dinner on the road for the year. We went to Palm Springs to one of the best restaurants in town. We ran into Bob Hope. What a thrill that was! I loved Bob Hope. I wanted to jump up and down and holler, but I didn't. I walked over quietly and asked him for his autograph. He was a nice gentleman and said, "Sure, honey," and gave me a great big kiss on the cheek and said, "You have a great dinner."

Carnival in the '60s

What a guy he was. He was a hero to the men serving in the military and to me. He was one of my favorite movie stars. A lot of actors and actresses could take some lessons from him. He was always giving up his personal time to go and cheer up the men fighting and protecting our country.

After the Indio fair, we were ready for our forty-five-day run without a day off. Artie would ask, "Sweetheart, do you have the rag ready?" "Yes, Artie, I have the rag ready," I would reply.

I had to keep a wet rag ready at all times to wash his face every two seconds to keep him awake for the ride to the next spot. The fairs were about thirty to seventy-five miles apart, and we were tired. It was very hard on us, but we had to keep going.

Sometimes we would be traveling in a lot of freezing rain. Then other times we were on long and curvy mountain roads. Many times we would tear down after a five- to ten-day spot, load up, and hit the road.

We often had a bottle going around, helping to keep us awake and keep the energy going so we could get to the next spot. Sometimes we only had five hours in between shows. It was time to rise and shine except we didn't have to rise because we didn't get to sleep on the trip. What a ride that was! Then we would put on our aprons and start working all over again.

We had a lot of drifters asking for jobs, and we were glad to have the help. We would all help each other. When the joints were down on the ground, we would jump in and get it done.

We had a rule not to drink before five p.m., which meant we were not alcoholics. I don't know who made up that rule, but we lived by it. We didn't believe in drugs to stay awake, so we did it the old fashioned way with willpower and alcohol.

Sometimes when the show was a little slow at the beginning of the season and there was no racetrack, the guys would go to their favorite trailer and get a card game going. They would invite some of the town folks.

One afternoon I was going back to my trailer to catch a little nap and all of a sudden people were yelling, "Raid! Raid! Get out." I turned around to look, and everybody was running out of a trailer parked in the back line-up. They were running all over the place trying to hide.

I heard the sirens and saw police cars pulling up. By then most everybody had either jumped into a joint and acted like they were working or had gone into a trailer or had jumped into their cars and drove off. The show sent out the patch man, which was Artie, to talk to the police, but they would not listen to him this time. Most of the time he could take care of anything and it didn't go any further.

But these police were there and they had their orders. They were going into the trailer and stopping everything going on. They came out with two guys I had seen on the midway many times—Jake from the spin game and Don from the water-shoot game.

After they were arrested, Artie had to go down to the police station and bail them out. What had happened was there were a couple of townspeople playing in the game, and I guess they lost quite a bit of money. They were going to get it back one way or the other. So I guess life goes on and sometimes it costs a little more money then you had planned on.

We went to Victorville and San Bernardino. Victorville was a nice little town with country folk.

"Artie, some day I would like to live in a small town like this," I said.

I really think Victorville was one of my favorite spots.

We got rained out three out of five days that year. It was windy, and it was very cold. Things were blowing all over the place, and it was hard to keep anything on the shelf. It felt more like a blizzard instead of April showers. It was really coming down.

But it was April showers working up to May flowers. I couldn't wait. I loved flowers. They bring a special joy to my heart.

We were going in the hole for that spot—not making money—so we had to spend the money we had made from the last spot. We had tucked away money to pay for the nut (the rent) and the rest of the expenses we owed the show.

No matter what spot we played, we got either one or two days for profit. So when we first started the season, we would only make money on an average of one out of three spots. Things would happen like trucks breaking down, or we would get rained out from a big storm.

"Phyllis, honey, today I want you to pick up the money and be the watcher," Artie said.

"Thanks, Artie," I would answer.

I would get to sit down and watch. It would still be fourteen to sixteen hours, but with lots of breaks. It was especially nice when it was a busy spot; I liked staying busy.

Cocktail hour was at five p.m. every day. There was no drinking until five, when I would meet my honey for dinner and cocktails. Most of the time, we had dinner together.

We always had a watcher because the people that worked in the joints were only supposed to take enough money out of their apron to eat with and nothing more. I was right there most of the time so I could tell what they had to eat. They didn't know who else was watching them.

I would make my collection every hour and watch all day to make sure they weren't taking off with the apron or taking more than a sandwich (so to speak). If they were caught doing anything else, they would get patted down. If they were found with a lot of extra money on them, they were in a lot of trouble. They would get beaten up and sometimes thrown off the show.

Meanwhile, Artie and the other owners were at the racetrack having a good time betting on the horses and having their cocktails in a nice air-conditioned room. While everyone else was working in 105-plus-degree weather.

I used to tell Artie my horses were on the midway and I could take my money home with me. I said he should try it some day. Of course he acted like I had never spoken a word. It was called the four-letter word "blind love" on my part.

I always remembered the bridge. My life had improved a great deal since then. I was proud he trusted me to take care of everything. But sometimes I wondered if it was working out fair between the two of us.

Once we were playing the Sacramento fair, and it was hot enough to fry an egg on the asphalt. It was 105 in the shade and

115 or more in the sun. We were making a lot of trips to the public showers to stay wet, clothes and all. It was the only way we could work in that kind of heat for sixteen hours or more. Sacramento was one of our best moneymakers for the season each year, and nobody wanted to miss out on this fair.

In the winter, Artie still had concessions on The Pike, and that took care of him for whatever he needed. There was more money on the road to be made, but The Pike helped out for the in-between time.

When we first started the season, we played with different shows. May is when the Foley and Burke show would start their season and when we would join them. We had a clown on the midway with us as soon as we connected to the Foley and Burke show. It certainly lightened up the midway, and the kids loved him. He had his funny-looking face and outfit and funny-looking balloons he made into animals. Then he would give them away free with candy suckers to the children. I think he had one of the most fun jobs on the midway.

Most everybody got their motels at the same place in each spot we played. What a party that was. Sometimes they would get kicked out and have to move in the middle of the night. But most of the time they got away with everything because there was too much money involved.

I bought the first motor home on the road. I wanted to make sure Brad had a place to call home. After everybody came into my motor home and saw how comfortable and convenient it was, everybody started buying motor homes and trailers.

Living on the lot keeps the thieves away at night. We even got hookups for our trailers in all the shows we worked. That's when you learn to appreciate water and electricity.

We had to learn to conserve. There were many times we got overloaded and didn't have any water or electricity. We didn't like it, but we would have to go to the public showers until we got everything going again. It was a pain. It took too much time away from our work.

One night we were playing the Pasadena fair, which was a busy fair. We were always tired after this fair. It was in the middle of the season, it was very hot weather, and it was about three weeks long.

One day I was walking to the trailer at the Pasadena fair to have a drink with Artie. I found Artie was already there having his drink in our nice air-conditioned motor home.

"The air conditioning is nice," I said to him. "I think I would like to stay right here for the rest of the day."

Artie said he was feeling a little faint, so he had come in a little early.

"Honey, why don't you take it easy until the sun goes down?" I suggested.

"OK, babe, I'll be right here if you need me," he said.

I gave him a big kiss and hug and said, "I will see you later, honey." I then went back to work after dinner and my two cocktails. It was nice because it had cooled off pretty well.

The bosses were the only ones allowed to have cocktails while the show was open. If any of the help got caught drinking on the job, they were in big trouble—beaten and thrown off the lot with no place to go. They could have been demoted to a different joint that didn't make as much money as the previous one.

Most everyone was far away from home and/or didn't have a home to go to. You had to take care of the only home most carnies ever had.

We went to the nurse's office at the beginning of every fair. It was located on the main lot of the fairgrounds. We had to get our vitamin B-12 shot for health and energy. The times were different in those days. The shot was free. They were actually out to help us and not out for the money. People were looking out for people.

We were feeling right uptown with those hook-ups. It was nice of them to put in those hook-ups for us at each spot where we played. The other ride jocks and concession workers slept under the rides or in the concessions behind the counters. It was pretty warm out that time of year, so it wasn't a problem. It was like camping out.

We were a tight family. It reminds me of the song, "We Are Family," especially the line, "I have my brothers and sisters with me," which was true for me, because most of my family went with us most of the time.

When we arrived at the Fresno fair, we were pretty tired, so we parked everything and went to the motor home and hit the sack. We were rested in the morning—must have gotten about seven hours of sleep. We smelled the coffee from the cook shack and couldn't wait to get some of Russ's coffee, some bacon and eggs, and his French toast. We were hungry and ready to go again. Russ and his wife, Ruth, were good cooks, and they were very clean. They always worked their own store, which was the cook shack. They would hire about six other people to work side-by-side with them.

You always knew the food was good and clean, which was important, since this was the main place to eat day after day. We arrived in the cook shack early that morning, and Russ decided to join us for a cup of coffee, as he did quite often. But this time he wanted to talk to Artie about something.

Russ was really upset that somebody had broken into his trailer the night before and had stolen his snow-cone mix, some of his Pepsi mix, four cases of Coke, and his lemonade mix. They had broken open his new trailer door, and now it wouldn't shut all the way.

Artie asked Russ, "Would you want me to send out the enforcers tonight? We'll get them to stay all night in your trailer, so if they come back we'll be able to catch them."

Russ was happy and thanked Artie over and over.

I was thinking, *You should have mercy on their souls if they dare to come back.* Our enforcers were pretty big and strong. At three a.m. there were four guys about fifteen years old working their way in the broken door. They were not with the show, but they still were met with a .45-caliber gun right in their faces. I'm sure it scared them. Then the enforcers called the police.

I would say those boys were pretty lucky. If it had been some of the carnies breaking in, they would have taken a beating and maybe got thrown off the lot, told to never come back again, and not been given their pay. That's a hard thing to deal with, especially when you're far away from home. That's what the enforcer did. I always tried not to be around when anything like that was going on. I couldn't stand any kind of violence. And believe me, there was enough going on in every spot we played.

When my son was approximately three years old, I told him if anybody ever tried to pick him up to start screaming, kicking, and punching whoever it was. The first person who picked him up after that was a policeman asking, "Are you lost, little boy? Where is your mommy?" This policeman was just trying to do his job, but my son started screaming, kicking, and punching like his mom had told him to do. You've never seen a more embarrassed policeman. It sounded like child abuse was going on. One of the show people told the policeman the child was with the show, and that settled everything down.

Just before every show we played, we always had a show meeting. It was to remind us that we were there to put on the show—and to put on our thinking caps and not to fight with anyone unless we really had to. We wanted to leave town on a good note so they would want us back the next year.

The people at the Pleasanton fair reminded me of when I lived in Kansas where I was born and lived as a child. They were not in a hurry and paid attention to what you were saying. They responded to you by looking into your eyes and answering you back. I thought, *Wow, this is pretty great.* I loved that little town of Pleasanton. They were the kind of people I had missed in my life, which life now had gotten a little too busy and fast for me. But as we say, life goes on and everything changes.

When we played the California State Fair in Sacramento, some of the rowdy customers were throwing firecrackers at us all day. This was a big celebration for the black people. It marked the day of freedom for them. It was the Fourth of July! We played the Sacramento fair in July each year. It was one of the biggest and hottest fairs we played. The people still came out to play the games and ride the rides and eat their cotton candy and drink their soda pops, even with the heat.

We weren't their favorite people in those days. Needless to say, I don't like the Fourth of July celebration anymore after my first year of working in Sacramento. We had to put all of our prizes in the back of the booth because there were so many different gangs there. They would come at once and try to steal everything at the same time.

One morning when we were having our breakfast in the cook shack, Artie saw a few guys trying to steal some food. All it took was for Artie to snap his fingers or put thumbs up for the enforcers to throw the bums out. That was after we fed them and told them if they needed jobs we would be glad to help them out. They said we are not looking for jobs. So we said "What's up with that?" Then we continued to throw the bums out. Luckily, we had our own enforcers—you could call them our own police force. We had them to protect us. We were secure with our own enforcers, and it was not a problem! Like I said, we were like any other town, but we had our little town on wheels.

We would always go to the best restaurant in town for dinner and would have at least one great meal in each fair we played. It was a lot of fun. We would get a chance to visit with each other. We didn't have much time when we were working. This was one of my best memories. Some of my unpleasant of memories are of a lot of different fights in all the different towns. In Reno there were the Indians, in Bakersfield there were the Mexicans, in San Jose there were the blacks and Mexicans, in Livermore there were the rednecks, in Pleasanton there were the country boys. There were many more, and then there were towns like San Jose and Sacramento where the police had everything under control, so we didn't have to fight.

Here are some of the big fairs we played: Phoenix, Bakersfield, Tulare, Victorville, Madera, San Bernardino, San Jose, Sacramento, Vallejo, San Mateo, Santa Rosa, Los Angeles, Pasadena, Livermore, Reno, Pleasanton, and Pomona.

CHAPTER 22

Snowstorm Breaks all Records Since 1890 and Thanksgiving

WELL, THE PHONE rang and brought me back to Coeur d'Alene, Idaho. I quit daydreaming about the carnival. I was watching the snow come down in my front yard. This was our second year with record-breaking snowfall. The first year broke all records since 1890.

Many of us were snowed inside our homes. I couldn't get out if I had to for any reason. I felt like I was being buried alive and hoped the roof didn't cave in on me to finish things off. The snow was covering half of my sliding glass door in the back of the house, and it was frozen shut. The front door was frozen shut and wouldn't budge. I had paid a roofer a couple of days earlier a couple of hundred dollars to clean off the roof so it wouldn't cave in on me. That took care of any chances of clearing the pathway to get out of the house. They didn't tell me the snow had to be put somewhere and it would be in front of my doorways and driveway. It kept snowing and snowing, and I didn't think it was going to quit. I was more trapped than ever.

I was trapped in the house for about three weeks. That's not a good feeling. I had never felt so helpless. Even if I could have gotten out, my car wouldn't have made it because the streets had not been plowed. The plow truck couldn't have gotten through the roads to have done anything. They were snowed in too. There were cars all over town that were stranded and not going anywhere.

Thank God I could see what was happening on the TV, and my heat and electricity were still working. My angels were there for sure, taking good care of me. People were stranded all over town. A lot of places were without heat and electricity for days. We were having a complete whiteout.

Suddenly the phone rang. It was my granddaughter, Erica, calling to tell me they finally had gotten out and were on there way over to help me. I was feeling very blessed, because Erica and Clifford, my grandson were my angels this time. Thank God for grandchildren.

Clifford brought his snow blower and cleared my driveway for me so I could get out if needed. I was certainly feeling better knowing I could get out of my house in case I got ill or if my house was on fire. It was a pretty scary time. I thanked my granddaughter and grandson and gave them a lot of hugs and kisses.

We were still in the middle of a snowstorm, and I wasn't going anywhere unless I had to. The morning passed, and the darkness was coming on for the evening. I was still in my house sitting in my comfy chair, staring out the window and watching the snow coming down. I will say it sure was a pretty sight to see.

When the snow stopped long enough, the snowplows came. Now we could get out of our house and get around. We started planning at whose house we were going to have Thanksgiving dinner in town. We weren't going to have it at the ranch up on the hill—way too much snow.

We settled on my other grandson Matt's and my granddaughter Gen's house. It was a good, central location. Their home was right in the middle of Coeur d'Alene. I cooked the ham and bought the green beans. My son, Brad, and daughter-in-law, Cheryl, were cooking the turkey and making the dressing. Everybody was bringing one or two different dishes for our Thanksgiving dinner. We always had nice holiday dinners together.

Snowstorm Breaks all Records Since 1890 and Thanksgiving

I was lucky to have such a real nice family. Here in Idaho, the town always has something going on for the holidays. In the beginning of December, we were getting ready to have our Christmas fireworks and light show in downtown Coeur d'Alene.

It's a spectacular show. I told a new neighbor who had moved into our neighborhood, "Make sure you don't miss this show. It is a great one. People come from miles around to see this show, so you sure don't want to miss it."

Then the phone rang. It was my girlfriend Sue who said, "Phyllis, let's go early so we can get a good seat at the Eagles, sitting at the window. Then we can stay nice and warm and still be able to see the light show."

"I would love to go early," I replied.

Good thing we did. There were only two seats left in front of the window and we grabbed them.

We had a few drinks while we were waiting, and again it was a great light show. We have always enjoyed the people at the Eagles, so all and all it was a great evening. We always took turns driving home, and it was my friend Susie's turn. She had only had one drink all evening. So my turn to party!

CHAPTER 23

Carnival Memories

I REMEMBER ONE day walking by a trailer in the back lineup of the show. It was real private area. Nobody ever went back there. I was taking a walk to get away for a short break when I overheard some guys talking about what happened at the track that day. It sounded like there were about six or seven guys. I'm not sure if they were making bets on the side for the horse races or not. I knew sometimes they did.

Then I overheard them talking about a jockey who had just been murdered.

Then next thing I heard was, "He should have known better. When you agree to throw a race you better do it. You don't mess around with those guys or you can see what happens."

I never walked by that trailer again. I didn't want to know who had been in there talking, and I didn't want them to know I had overheard anything.

When there was a large amount of money being bet, something was definitely going on. I didn't want to know. At the time, we were playing the Pomona fair with a big racetrack nearby. There was a lot of money being spent at the track. I walked away quietly and never went back to that spot again.

I never said anything to anybody. Not even my boyfriend, Artie, because I wasn't sure if he knew any of the guys in the trailer.

Now I should tell you about out secret language. "Joints" were concessions, "nut" was rent. We would talk in carny when we didn't want anyone to know what we were talking about. We would drop the first letter of each word and add "kis" to the front ("kisarney" was the word "carney"). It took a little practice but it was fun.

There was other carny lingo. "Ace" or "a single" was a one-dollar bill, "deuce" was a two, "a fin" was a five, "a sawbuck" was a ten-dollar bill, "a double" was a twenty-dollar bill, "a one-half of yard" was a fifty-dollar bill, and "a yard" was a hundred-dollar bill. "DQ" was short for disqualified; "end" was to get paid your end for a day's work. We always got paid every day. "Fix" or "ice" meant to give protection money. "First on the right" meant the first location on the midway or the first hole on the right, which was considered the best location. "Flag" or "flags up" meant the cook shack was open. "Flash" meant how you decorated your joint, such as with big teddy bears. The "G" was the trailer after the show closed for gambling. The gambling trailer was supposed to be open only for the carnies on the show. The "G" trailer also had a combined convenience store, bar, snack stand, and casino. They played mostly cards and dice games.

The "patch guy" was someone who took care of all beefs, disagreements, misunderstandings, unhappy customers, and the police department. He's the guy who went ahead of the show and took care of any problem with booking before we got there. We would say, "Everything is good. The patch is in."

"We blanked out" meant we didn't make any money in that spot. "Gadget girl show" was slang for a "g-string" (strip show) that in some places was open to the public and sometimes was an after-hours show just for the carnies. "Beef" was an argument with the crowd or a disagreement. "Going south" was stealing money. "Goon Squad"—on some shows—was a gang of the tougher guys who acted as enforcers. "Grab joint" or "grease joint" was an eating concession. "Green help" were inexperienced workers. "Grind store" was usually a small game that needed a lot of action to make a profit, like a dime pitch. "Hanky Pank" was a game where every player won a prize every time—a five-cent prize dispensed for every fifty cents played.

That's some of the carny lingo.

CHAPTER 24

Back to Idaho and Sunday Get-Togethers

THE PHONE RANG and brought me back to Idaho. It was my, son, Brad, reminding me to pick up the cake and bring it to the ranch by noon on Sunday. Our family gets together every Sunday, but this Sunday was special—a birthday party for one of the grandchildren.

The ranch is our property on a great mountain with the famous Coeur d'Alene Lake right on the other side. If you went to the top of our property, you could see this lake with beautiful pine trees surrounding it. We have a nice creek, running right on one side of our property, that runs all year long just absolutely beautiful.

How blessed I am. This is something I had wanted all my life. When you're there, it's like you have gone back in time about fifty years. It's very quiet, and you cannot see the main road from the house because the pine trees surround you. On this beautiful day, the sun was streaming down on our mountain. You could only hear the birds chirping and the deer talking to each other or see the turkey walking by.

The good Lord has blessed me with another day to enjoy. He has given me this beautiful mountain to live on and help take care of. I can't thank Him enough. Brad and my daughter-in-law, Cheryl, live there all year long. They have a couple of pigs and some chickens, and the fresh eggs are great.

I put a fifth-wheel trailer up on the property. It's thirty-three feet with two tip-outs, so there's plenty of room in it. It has the septic, electric, and well hooked up. I like to go up in the summer and hang out and have barbecues with the family. The winter can be a little rough with the snow and ice on our private road. The kids are up for it, but my pleasure is in the summer.

We have an apple orchard, a plum orchard, peach tree, pear tree, cherry tree, raspberry bushes, and blackberry bushes. Also, my brother, Ronnie, and his wife, Sammie, have added to the landscape. They have their trailer at the very top of our property. They come down to watch the ballgames with Brad and Cheryl on Sundays. They also join us when we are having our family get-togethers. We have a lot of family time—something I had always wanted. All in all, life is pretty good. We are happy to go hang out at the ranch.

We all enjoy a lot of barbecues with Brad and Cheryl and driving the six-wheel Gator around that can take you all over the property in no time at all. When I first saw the property, it was in the dead of winter, the snow was pretty thick, and the ice was bad. I never would have gone to see this property in the winter, but it was in foreclosure. I figured it was going to be a good deal, and it was. It reminded me of the five-acre property in Sacramento. That had one hundred years of junk on it, but this one only has fifty years of junk.

The electricity was turned off. The sellers had a barbecue in the middle of the living room for their cooking and heat. That was a pretty sad thing to see. It gets below zero every winter here. I don't know how they could have lived that way. It was in bad shape and needed a tune-up that was going to cost a lot of money and a lot of work. I really did like the challenge to make it livable and beautiful. I'm sure a lot of people would have turned down this property at the first look-see. People could not see past the mess and were not willing to do all the work that was needed to be done. I loved the location and knew it could be a nice piece of property, so I went for it. It was also priced right!

Back to Idaho and Sunday Get-Togethers

I could see my life's dream coming true. I knew our work was cut out for us, but I didn't care, and it didn't scare me off. All I could think of was, "I'm home, Lord. You have done it again." I thought I was in heaven.

I bought the property in 2001. It took me five to six years to get the major things accomplished. I had to work with the money that came in and do the repairs as I could afford them, a little at a time. Brad helped out with a lot of the repairs.

Things have changed a lot since then, and the property is beautiful. We are enjoying it very much. I retired from the convenience store and the Texaco gas station, so I now have more time to enjoy the ranch.

CHAPTER 25

Thinking About the Carnival and Watching the Snow

IT'S A COLD, beautiful, white winter, and I'm sitting in my comfortable chair again, staring out the window and remembering the days in the carnival.

Sometimes Artie would let me have a machine-gun game to run and keep half the profits, which was a nice added income for me. We made as much, if not more, than doctors and lawyers in those days. That was pretty good income. Everything is different today. The carnies and show owners don't make as much as we did. Everybody has their hands in your pocket these days, getting their piece of your action.

With the machine-gun game, sometimes I would put a stool against the counter and put an apron on Brad. He loved it. He would work about five or six hours. Everybody loved him—he always had a smile for everyone. He was good at loading the rifles and asking for the money. He was also good at making change. I, of course, was right there for any questions and whatever came up.

Brad always had a good time playing all the games. He liked the machine-gun and ball games the best, and he loved all the rides. Brad had a big backyard to play in, the whole fairgrounds. It was quite educational.

The show was a good place to bring up your children. They learned how to be responsible and "honor thy neighbor." They all learned you only get money after the job is done and you don't spend more than you make. We didn't have the crime that we have today, so the kids could run around free. It's not like the crime today with people shooting each other and children getting into drugs. That has hurt our country and our young people. Drugs have caused so much trouble in so many different ways. It's a really sad thing when you can remember how much better life could be.

I think people have lost their way. They need to go back to church and teach their children about God and His teaching. They need to learn to love and treat each other the way they would like to be treated. It would be nice to get back to having integrity and helping each other have a better life. That's how my generation grew up—with morals, integrity, and caring for the other people in our world. Money was not everything, and money did not rule like it does with a large percentage of people now.

At the end of eleven years, Artie gave me my own unit to run at a different location. He gave me four different concessions: a balloon game, a ball game, a machine-gun, and a basketball game. It was a lot of fun having my own unit, and a lot of hard work, but I enjoyed it. It was for only one spot. but I was really happy about it!

I guess we were going to be apart for a little while, which was different for us. We hadn't been apart for more than two days ever since we had gotten together eleven years earlier. I think he must have trusted me more as time went on. Wow, what a concept.

I had twelve people who went with me, and I put three agents in each store. We brought a lot of stuffed animals with us and had to re-order some more while we were there. This means I was pretty busy, and I was making money. The big trucks would follow the shows around because we couldn't carry the extra stuffed animals and other prizes that we would need, especially in the good spots.

We had real good weather and stayed busy, and everybody worked really well together. Artie was surprised that we did so good. I was still wondering why he let me go on my own. I thought maybe this was the beginning of the end for us. I was going to try one more time to get him to give up the road and buy an arcade in some nice town. It didn't matter where it was going to be.

I wanted to stay in one spot. I thought it was time to get my son off the road. Brad was becoming a teenager, so I thought we should be living a simpler life. It would be better for him. I didn't know how it was going to work out, but I was going to give it my very best.

Artie didn't take me up on my offer. I was really disappointed. He was my love, strong shoulder, and my strength. It was going to break my heart to make the changes that I was going to make. I knew what I had to do. It was a seven-day spot and we were real busy. I made a lot of money on my new adventure—enough for me to call it quits! It was the end of the season. This was the last spot, and it was going to be my last spot forever. I was not going back.

I didn't like what I saw for my future. I was a happy type of person. I would have stayed that way if I could have stayed naive about all the things that were really going on. But I guess I had to grow up at some point and see the truth of how things were going on around me.

It really spoiled things when I learned about the different trailers and what was really going on. I was so heartbroken. I had to make some real changes in my life. You can't go back to the way it was when things have changed right in front of you. Once you understand there were just too many lies, you wonder what has ever been real or true.

These things forever broke my heart. I don't know if I ever will get over them completely. I have only learned to live with the pain of it all.

This was my chance to get a new life. Don't get me wrong, I still loved my Artie very much. But I could see the writing on the wall, and it didn't look good for me. And it was not going to be an emotionally healthy life for me to continue that way.

By then I had begun to see things differently. Life is about lots of lessons. I had learned about the sex trailers that were always on the lot for the men to enjoy. These were the extra women they would pick up at each spot we played. I thought there were only gambling trailers for the men, which I thought already took up enough of all the men's time. Ha! I was surprised with the news of the trailers. Some of the new agents on the lot let the cat out of the bag, talking about when they were getting their breaks, that they were going to go to trailer number six for their daily quickie, and how they had to get a draw before they left.

Also, Artie was actually married with two children. I didn't care about this for a long time, but after a bit of time you do start to care. Artie and I were together all summer and we would get together for four nights every week in the winter. I would cook for three nights a week and then he would take me out one night a week. His wife didn't mind, she had her own boyfriend that was a dentist.

We were a happy couple and we got along well. Of course, I didn't know what was going on behind the scenes. I learned to be a good listener and smile a lot. But then the years went by, and I started looking at the security in my life, and there was no future there for me.

With the new information I had picked up on and all the things going on around me, it was a lot easier to leave. I had tried to get Artie to settle down in one town. I was trying to get a fun little carnival of our own or an arcade game, but he was not interested. I had to make my move and take care of my son and me. Nobody else was going to.

Artie's Italian family was old-fashioned. Until the father died, nobody could get a divorce. This was another thing bothering me. It was adding up, and I was having a hard time seeing clearly. I know it was becoming more painful to be where I was. I didn't want to live in pain anymore. I had to make a move.

I had met Artie's wife once. She had come on the road with her dentist friend to check me out. That's what I was told anyway.

She came right up to the booth where I was working and spoke to me. She said hello and asked if I could please get Artie for her. I said, "Sure, who should I say is asking for him?"

She said, "His wife" and she would like to get some ride tickets for the kids. I thought she was nice and she certainly was well dressed and pretty.

Artie and his wife were waiting for his father to pass so they could get a divorce. The oldest daughter was also waiting. Nobody wanted to upset Artie's father.

Thinking About the Carnival and Watching the Snow

I understand a lot more now. I'm sure there was a nice inheritance with some terms hanging over their heads. I heard five years after I left the show that Artie's father died and Artie and his wife did get a divorce and she married her dentist boyfriend.

In the winter, I would sell stuffed animals in Long Beach. I had for about five years. This was also my last year of selling stuffed animals on the corners of different gas stations forty-five days before Christmas. I went to Los Angeles with my motor home and filled it with stuffed animals so full that I had to get inside the motor home so they could finish completely filling it up. I did this for about four or five trips—back and forth to Los Angeles to the supplier we used in the summertime for the carnival.

Then I brought them to my house in Long Beach. When I got home, I had to climb out the window on the driver side to get out of the motor home. I completely filled my house with different kinds of stuffed animals. We didn't have any walking space by the time I got done. I certainly didn't want to go back and forth, and I didn't have the time. Los Angeles was too far, and it would have been hard to do in the middle of doing all the work and the hours I had to put in selling all day long.

The best thing to do was to treat my house as a warehouse and buy everything up front. Then I would start talking to different gas station owners, offer them a cut, get a yes, and then get set up. I loaded my motor home with a different variety of stuffed animals and then go back and forth to my home and pick up more animals and bring them back to the location where we were working.

I brought a TV for Brad so he could watch his cartoons. There was food in the refrigerator, books to read, and a change of clothes. We had a generator in the motor home so we could take showers anytime, but we waited until everything was closed down at night. We closed the curtains and pack the stuffed animals into the motor home at night, which gave us little room to get around, but we lived with it.

We watched a little TV and then retired and started again the next morning. When we started to get low in inventory, we had to unplug our electricity and our water hook-ups and travel down the road to our home to get more stuffed animals.

I'm sure some people thought we would be an easy mark to rob, so here's how it went. I guess I fooled them a bit. We only had one situation that was unpleasant. A couple of men came up and tried to rob me. They had a knife in their hands. They asked me for my money, and I said, "You don't want to do this. You'll be sorry. Just walk away, and we can forget the whole thing. This money was for my son and me, and it has to last for the whole winter to pay our rent and to buy food."

"Lady," one of them said, "we came here to take your money home with us, and that's what we intend to do. So hand over the money in your apron, and whatever you have inside the trailer, and we won't harm you or your son."

So I did what I was taught—I acted crazy and brought out my gun from my pocket. It was a .38-caliber short-nose pistol. I shot two shots up in the air, and I said to the guys, "Next time it will be for you. Now get the hell out of here and don't come back." I was screaming at them by that time. I had learned how to be a good bluffer from traveling with the carnies.

Sometimes I thought I had no brains—just guts, which did get me through quite often.

"The next time, I will not have any conversations with you," I added. "I'll start shooting, and I'll get away with it because it will be self-defense."

I was a woman with her small child trying to make a living. How could I go wrong? I thought those men were going to hurt my son and me.

I got scared and started shooting.

"I think that would sound real good to any judge. Don't you think so?" I asked.

I never saw them again. I'm sure I was called "the crazy lady," and that's what I wanted to be called. It works every time.

Thinking About the Carnival and Watching the Snow

It probably would not work today. Things are a little different. They would probably shoot me. I was not about to give up the money to support my son and me for the winter.

We would make three thousand to four thousand dollars a year. Pretty good for forty-five days' work. It was a lot of fun to sell them at a discount price and sell the heck out of them like we did. People never could afford them in the department store. They were real happy to see us come each year. They had to find us, because we were at a different location each year. I liked knowing those children were going to get a stuffed animal that year for Christmas.

The gas station owner was asked not to allow us to be there again because the shopping center didn't like us cutting into their action. Most of the time they didn't get fined or in trouble. So we always went to a new location each year.

My son Brad and my niece Angie helping me sell stuffed animals on the corner at Christmas time. Both kids were 11 years old in 1976.

The city inspector seemed to always find us, but they never stopped us, and he never fined me either. They just asked us not to do it again. Every year it was the same city inspector, and every year he would just give me a warning. I don't think he really minded. I think he felt like we wouldn't be there if we didn't need the money to survive or have a nice Christmas. He bought some of our stuffed animals for his children each and every year.

I sat on the corner with my son for about five years every Christmas. It was fun moving around. We would get into different neighborhoods, and we would have a new market each year that increased sales. I really enjoyed it, and my son had a good time. We always made sure we brought his bicycle. Brad stayed pretty busy and enjoyed the people coming and going.

This was in a time when there weren't many discount stores around, so we were well appreciated because our stuffed animals were twenty dollars cheaper than at the stores. It helped our sales a lot. I'm sure a lot more kids got a nice teddy bear from Santa all the years we were sitting on those corners.

CHAPTER 26

Torrance, California, to Cave Junction, Oregon, and the Yellow Submarine

MY BROTHER, RONNIE, moved to Cave Junction, Oregon. It was in the middle of the summer, and he was on his way to Oregon, when he stopped by my house. Ronnie said, "I'm done with my yellow submarine. It's completed and ready to go."

He had built his yellow submarine in the backyard of our Torrance family home. He had taken a twenty-eight-foot trailer, for which he paid only a hundred dollars, and made a great living quarters out of it with a nice wood stove inside.

On the outside, he made it look like a yellow submarine. He put three transmissions in his Iron Horse truck with twenty-four gears in it—whatever that means. He made the famous magazine *Four Wheeler* for having an outstanding artistic trailer and an outstanding truck.

We lived in a nice middle-class subdivision. I guess you know the neighbors were a little unhappy about the noise and how things were looking with the construction going on. I'm sure they were glad to see him leave.

When my brother left California, he came by to visit me one last time while I still lived in Long Beach.

"Phyllis, I am leaving, and we may never see each other again," he said, "and I want you to understand how great marijuana is for you. Please try this for me before I go."

The Carnival Girl

My brother Ronnie's truck and trailer, which he designed based on lyrics from the popular Beatles song, "Yellow Submarine," was featured in *Four Wheeler* magazine.

Ronnie begged me to try one marijuana cigarette.

"Ronnie, you know I don't like marijuana," I said.

"Phyllis, if you could do me this little favor," he suggested.

"OK, Ronnie, just this one time. It seems to mean so much to you." I did, and I did not like it at all. First I started laughing uncontrollably. Then I thought there were snakes under the furniture in my house.

I never tried that again, and I thought everybody who smoked marijuana must be a little strange. Why would they want to feel so different and not be in the real world? I still do not smoke and never did smoke marijuana again. But I understand it is being used for sick patients, and I assume it really helps them.

You never know how things are going to turn out. There is always change in the air. My brother had gone hippie all the way with free love, drugs, living off the land, and being against the government for all its lies. He sold the house he inherited from my grandpa and grandma, went to Oregon, and bought twenty areas in Cave Junction.

Torrance, California, to Cave Junction, Oregon, and the Yellow Submarine

Before he left, he made a cave out of the home in Torrance. I wish I had a picture of his creation. You would not have known you were not in a cave. He used plaster, and it felt and looked real—he had created a different look for sure. He did different things such as hanging his bed from the ceiling with four big chains. That must have been real different to sleep in. He had his dresser and a chair hanging from the ceiling with some chains too.

The windows were small and round and they looked like they were windows from a boat. My brother had that idea before builders did. It looked pretty cool. In the kitchen, he had everything hanging from the ceiling: the silverware, the skillets, and the pots and pans. Maybe my brother was in a different world at the time.

He sold that house to his buddy. His buddy didn't mind living in a cave, because he had helped him build it. About two months later, the house burned down—the good news was nobody got hurt. I believe there was a little LSD involved with the construction and destruction of the cave.

When my brother got to Cave Junction and bought his twenty-acre property, there were some rich hippies on the mountain above his property. They were there for the same reason: to live off the land and go back a hundred years in time.

That's where the parties were. His neighbors had a cement dance floor, a swimming pool, and a spa. When my brother invited me up to visit him, I thought it was going to be interesting, but it went a lot further then that. There was marijuana in the brownies, LSD in the cakes, and a lot of different kinds of drugs in the food. Ronnie was kind enough to tell me, so I did not eat any of the food. He told me what was OK and what was not OK.

The town had one small grocery store, one post office, and of course, one bar and restaurant. The hippies from the big cities were moving into paradise. They had pioneer spirits, and they wanted to start over again. They wanted to create a new world of love and peace, which I thought was a good idea. Too bad it didn't work out. I guess there was too much greed in our world, and there still is. Nobody ran the town—the people living there could do anything they were big enough to do. Ronnie lived on his twenty acres in his yellow submarine until he talked my uncle and me into purchasing the twenty acres below him. There was a cute little cabin on the twenty acres, and my brother built a second floor to the cabin, which made it a two-story—right uptown!

My brother was a real handyman—he could build anything. When we went to visit, it was a lot more comfortable since he built the upstairs. We were right uptown with a two-story cabin. We had lots of sleeping space with our new addition. This cabin was cute as a bug. It had a good wood stove in it, so we kept nice and toasty.

Ronnie said, "Sis, I had poison ivy for the first nine months I moved to Oregon. So don't go out and walk around by yourself. If you want to go anywhere, let me know and I'll go with you. I know how to handle the snakes and other animals around here, and I don't want you to get hurt."

"Hey, brother," I replied, "believe me, I won't go anywhere without you."

Phyllis and a friend crossing over the Oregon river, up in the air on a cable car, to get to our property in O'Brien, Oregon, in 1980.

Torrance, California, to Cave Junction, Oregon, and the Yellow Submarine

I knew I could never live in Cave Junction. It was a little too rugged for me. To even get to our property you had to take a cable car to cross over the river. You had to pull the wires yourself to get across. The forest rangers had built it, and they were nice enough to let us use it. The only other way to get to the property was when the river was low enough to cross, which only happened about two months a year. The cable car was the main path.

My granddaughter getting into the cable car, to get across the river to our property in O'Brien, Oregon, in 1990.

Ronnie got in a little trouble when he decided to join a partner in growing marijuana. They found a good place on the property and started working the land, digging the holes to do their planting. Then a telephone company employee was working on some telephone lines nearby. He could see the places where they were going to plant their pot.

My brother saw him up on the pole and said, "We better change our plans and not plant there. We'll have to cool it for a while. We have been found out."

The plants were on my brother's property, and he did not want to lose it.

Andy, the partner, got angry and decided to chase my brother out of town. He said my brother was trying to keep everything for himself. Andy decided to tell everybody in town he was going to waste ("shoot") Ronnie.

My brother decided to start carrying his .45-caliber pistol with him. The next day, Ronnie was working on his girlfriend's car in her driveway when Andy drove up. He started cursing at my brother again, which he had done many times all over town. My brother said he couldn't take it anymore.

Every place my brother went, there was Andy cursing him out, day after day. My brother told Andy to shut up or go for it. Andy was crazy enough to pull his gun out and start to shoot at my brother. But Ronnie was a little faster than Andy and shot him instead.

Ronnie said, "Sis, that was the scariest thing I had ever felt. My adrenaline was going as fast as it could go. I thought my heart was going to pop right out of my chest at any second. I went over to see how he was, because he fell right to the ground after I shot him. I still was a little scared, but I walked over to him and he wasn't moving. I put my hand on his neck to feel his pulse like in the movies and there was nothing so I knew right then he was dead. I had shot him dead with my .45-caliber pistol."

I went right into shock at the moment he told me that. I thought, *Oh my, that could have easily been Ronnie!*

Ronnie said it was nothing like he had every felt before or since that day. He said he was mixed with lots of fear and runaway energy. Also, he had thought of how living years ago must have been, when guns were in charge of people's lives. He said it felt like he was back in those days.

"I was feeling out of it. I didn't even know who I was at the time," he said.

My brother said he had nightmares for a long time after that. He said it's something you never get over, taking another person's life.

"Sis, it certainly wasn't how I wanted it to be and I was surprised it went so far," Ronnie said. "I have to pray about it and ask God to please forgive me."

Torrance, California, to Cave Junction, Oregon, and the Yellow Submarine

I felt bad that somebody had died, and of course I didn't know what to do to help my brother.

Artie had gotten the phone call about the shooting and came out on the midway to get me so he could tell me the news. We were playing the show at Fresno, which was one of our bigger fairs we played each year, so we couldn't leave.

Artie said, "We have to send him some money for a lawyer. I know a lawyer, and I will call him and make an appointment for Ronnie. Not to worry. I'll take care of things."

I was so pleased he said that, because I didn't know what to do.

Artie knew a judge in Medford and told the lawyer to try to have the trial there. He was a pretty nice judge who Artie said would give Ronnie a fair trail. Ronnie pleaded guilty due to self-defense.

The trial did end up in Medford, and my brother got five years on a suspended sentence and five years of probation. He only spent ten days in jail. I'm sure it helped that this was the first time he ever had been in trouble. Also, having a good lawyer and a fair judge helped. We wrote letters to the judge to let him know what we knew and thought about our brother, and Artie put in a good word for him.

Everybody in town testified for Ronnie and said Andy had told everybody he was going to waste my brother. My brother wasn't looking for any trouble and was innocent. Artie always knew how to handle things.

My family and I were lucky to have my Artie around. He was a great guy and smart, and he knew his way around.

Then we had another little incident. One of my nephews decided to bring a car that was not his and hide it on our property. By the time I heard about it and was getting ready to tell him to take his problems elsewhere, the sheriff showed up. It didn't take long before they caught up with him. I was afraid we would get into trouble because we owned the land. But we didn't.

My nephew had to pay back the money for the vehicle and do some time and that was it. I don't know what he was thinking when he did that.

Then there was my Uncle Russ who had already spent a lot of time in the jailhouse for robbery. He was a Navy Seal, also called

"Frogman" in those days, and they had taught him how to crack safes. He would deep-sea dive to sunken ships, open the safes, and deliver the goods to the captain.

But it was a problem that he knew how to crack safes. After the Navy, when he was broke and had a drink or two in him, he would fall back on what he knew best: cracking safes.

The problem was these were other people's private business safes, not a sunken Navy ship. So it was not OK, and he had to do some time for his mistakes. This always got him in a lot of trouble, and he was really glad when they changed the safes to the new combos. He didn't know how to get into them.

Uncle Russ was half Indian. He showed it when he was drinking, and then he was sorry when he got sober.

He was always in a lot of trouble with the law. He was known as one of the biggest bootleggers in the hills of Arkansas with his daddy, Ray Frost. Uncle Russ showed me lots of newspaper articles of the Frost family. They sold their alcohol and bootlegged in the hills of Arkansas—and went to jail a lot.

At one point my Uncle Russ took my brother, Ronnie, on train rides, jumping on and off and living in the boxcars. They went from city to city and state to state, living free like the hobos lived in those days. Uncle Russ followed the farm-picking route, going from farm to farm. He showed my brother how to live without working a regular job in town. My uncle called it "free living." He showed my brother that no matter what, he would never have to go hungry.

They told me stories about how they lived with real hobos at campsites. They called it "hobo jungle." When they slept at night, they took off their shoes and tied them to their feet to make sure they would have shoes in the morning.

Ronnie said, "Sis, it something you would only do once in your lifetime."

He said it was adventurous and he was glad he had done it. But he said he would never want to live that way again.

CHAPTER 27

Changing My Life

I WANTED TO change my life, so I started trying everything I could. I first tried to be a secretary, but my spelling was not good and my handwriting was about the same.

I thought real hard and figured it out. I wanted to work with the public, giving some kind of service to people in some form or another—help people have a better life somehow and make good money.

The light bulb went on. Real estate! It changed my whole life. It didn't come easy. I had to study hard. I didn't go to college, because it would have taken too long. I paid for a class at a private school for real-estate training. In a short time I was ready to go.

I had heard the licensing test was really tough to pass. A lot of people took the test two or three times. I was ready to take it as many times necessary for me to pass. I wanted a new career, and I was going for it.

In 1978 I took the test and passed it the first time. As soon as I received my license, I was making plans to move to Sacramento from Long Beach. The next year, I made my move.

The next step was a little surprising. It takes a while before you sell anything, and then it takes a while before you close your escrow.

This means no paycheck until you close escrow. About four to five months was the average wait time before receiving any money.

I was thinking, *Oh, what do I do now?* I wouldn't ask any of my family for help. That was not in the cards for me. I never ask anyone for help. I believed in the old-fashioned way—you pay your own way in life, and you make your own bed, so now you have to lie in it.

I had to hock my car until I got paid on my first sale. I went a little hungry for a short time—not my son, me—but it worked out in the long run. I would make sure he had good, healthy meals. I would buy him a steak, and I would buy me a beer (as my Uncle Russ used to say, there is a pork chop in every can!). I do remember telling my son I needed to buy him a pair of pants, so we would have to eat macaroni and cheese and potatoes and beans for that month.

Brad had it backward—he was born an adult. Now I'm waiting for him to revert to being a child. He was so understanding and so grown up. I didn't have that kind of understanding when I was his young age. I was so proud of him.

My mother, my sister and her three children, my son, and I moved to Sacramento to be close to my uncle who was so dear to us. At that time my mother was done trying to find Mr. Right. She wanted to be with her family, and we loved her very much. I was glad to have her back with us. So here we all went—my mother, my son, my sister and her three children, and I—to our new life.

We arrived in Sacramento on a Sunday afternoon. It was a nice, sunny day and a good day to get acquainted with and enjoy our new surroundings. We stayed with my Uncle Russ and his wife, Shirley. Shirley wasn't too happy to see us. We were there for about thirty days before we found a place of our own. I found a duplex for Brad and me, and my mom and my sister found apartments next door to each other downtown.

We lived close to each other. We would get together for Sunday lunches and play a few horseshoe games, card games, etc. The weather was always pretty nice in Sacramento, so we could do a lot of activities outside all year long. My Uncle Russ would take the boys fishing in the Sacramento River, and they really enjoyed themselves. We sure did get a lot of fresh fish. We also got a lot of fresh fruit from Uncle Russ's fruit trees. He had apples, pears, plums, and peaches, and he had grapevines with red and green grapes. They were mighty good.

My Uncle Russ had a great vegetable garden. I learned a lot. I hoped someday I'd have time to have a nice garden and maybe some fruit trees. My Uncle Russ really enjoyed having family around.

When the Sacramento State Fair came to town, I knew how to get everybody in the gates free. I went to the service gate and told them I was "with it." If they asked me any questions, I knew which spot they had just played and whose name to drop.

Even though I had quit the carnival, I said we were there to work. I figured it was a little white lie. It sure gave the kids more money to spend at the carnival, so the kids could have more fun things to do.

I bought a nice half-acre country home right in town. It was an old house but in good shape. It looked like an old Southern home where rich people lived in the South before the war. It really had its own charm. I loved it. It was a two-bedroom home with a great room for the living room and the dining room combined, and it had a giant kitchen almost as big as the great room. It had a big backyard and lots of trees. I put in a beautiful pool with a waterfall. I designed the backyard like I was living in Hawaii. It only took me three minutes to get to work from there, which was perfect.

While in the real estate office with Jack at Century 21, the office joke was "train, train, plus training." The first two years, I was the top agent and won a free trip to Las Vegas with another gal from a different Century 21 office in our same town. We had a blast. Everything was paid for. We were even given extra money to gamble. We figured we must have done real well for our offices to be treated so well. Life was definitely good to us, and we were happy!

My angels were always working with me and for me. I couldn't leave home without them. I would work the day and night shift and tend to the phones. I had all the buyers I wanted. They would get home from work and check the paper and call on all of our ads.

I was a live person to answer their calls—no answering service, not at this Century 21 real estate office at night. That's all it took to have a lot of business: being available and ready to service them. It was the key to the golden gate of success.

I also walked the streets with my son and his school friends and handed out flyers. Brad would get about four or five of his friends to help us, and I would give them some spending money. This was called my "farm" in the real estate business. I was farming it up pretty well.

This was getting information out about the neighborhood to potential buyers and sellers—what had sold, what was on the market, how much it was listed for, or what it had sold for. That gave people updated information about how things were going in the market and in their neighborhood. They loved the real-estate news from the newsletter. They said they would definitely call me to take care of their business when it was time.

The market was booming. It was 1979, and investors were coming out of the walls. They were buying everything. We would put a home on the market and have three or four different buyers fighting over the same property. This was good! I realized I should have done real estate a long time ago.

But in the early part of 1982 things slowed down almost to a halt. Emotions were running high, and we went into total fear. I was saying to myself, *What now?* We had house payments, car payments, credit-card debt, and everyday expenses. We had to scramble to get into something else so we could survive.

This is when I got very sick. I'm sure it was stress. I was starting to sleep about twenty hours a day and could not stay awake.

We had a real estate agent in our office, Tom, who had some big investors with big money. We thought he really had it made because he was making a lot of money—so much more than any of us. I am talking over a million dollars in a very short time. That was pretty shocking.

But Tom's investors were not happy. One morning when I walked into the office, they were having a screaming debate and stopped talking when they saw me. I heard them say they wanted to know when they were going to get their money back. Tom said it would happen, but it would be about three to four years before the market would turn over. He went on to explain further. It sounded like he was repeating himself over and over. You could tell he was very nervous and was running out of things to say.

I didn't know this kind of thing could ever happen. I'd only been selling real estate for about four years. But I understood we just had to be patient, and it would all turn around in the next three or four years.

I don't know how much money they were talking about, but it sounded like they couldn't or weren't willing to wait three or four years. I saw Tom was going to have to come up with a different idea for them somehow. They wanted their money back sooner—like right then.

When we came in the office the next morning, Tom wasn't there. We were wondering how things had gone with his investors. We didn't hear a thing all day long, and he didn't come into the office the whole day. That was unusual because Tom was always in the office working. We got a hold of his wife, and she said she hadn't heard from him all day and he was not answering his phone.

The next morning we read about Tom being found in his car trunk. The whole car had been burned to the ground. Oh, this was horrible. He had a wife and two kids.

I guess you shouldn't be handing other people's money unless you can give them all the facts.

The sad part was that Tom, like most of us, didn't have the facts. That could have been any of us greenhorns. There were all kinds of businesses closing down quickly and leaving town. It's like they came for the boom and now they were all done and were going away.

I knew this other guy named Mike. He had a used car lot and got involved with the wrong people. They were paying him five thousand dollars every time they used his name to put a mortgage together for buying a house. Whenever he could get somebody else to use his or her name, he would receive another five thousand dollars. He asked me if I wanted in, and I said a big no. I told him

I didn't want to do anything illegal, because in the long run it doesn't pay off.

"Mike, you are probably getting in over your head," I said. "You better be thinking about exactly what you are doing."

The next day my friend Gloria said, "Phyllis, let's grab a sandwich for lunch at our local coffee shop."

That's when I ran into Mike. His car lot was right across the street from our real estate office and around the corner from the coffee shop. We always were running into Mike at the coffee shop, but this time it was different.

"Phyllis, I'm in a lot of trouble and you were right," he told me. "I'm leaving town, and I wanted to say goodbye. I'll probably never see you again. I'm in a big hurry. I have to get out of town now."

He started walking away. Mike and I were really good friends and might have become more than that.

"Mike," I said, "I'm real sorry. I'll miss you. Please take care of yourself."

I don't know if he made it out of town or not, but I never saw Mike again. He had walked away from his car lot. He left everything there—his business papers and all kinds of things were still in his office. They said it looked like he had walked away from his house too. They didn't see a lot of his clothes missing from his closets. He didn't have a family, so we couldn't get any info from them. Nobody ever saw Mike again.

Another of my friends had bit the dust. Crime doesn't pay. It makes you feel really sad when you see your friends in so much trouble and you can't help them.

Through the grapevine I heard there was a mortgage company, a real estate company, and an appraiser's company that had come to the Sacramento area at the same time. They even had their own title company. They came for the boom, and they were now leaving at the same time. I heard they were creating some make-believe contracts and backing them up with their own appraisals, and then turning around and getting loans on them.

These loans were for three-hundred thousand dollars and up, and the addresses they were using did not exist. We had very few homes that would ever appraise for three-hundred thousand dollars in the Sacramento area, so they were definitely playing with fire. These people created a lot of trouble for themselves, and it came back their way. It was a big scam. They had to get out of town in a hurry because the FBI and lots of people were looking for them. I'm real sorry that some of my friends got a little greedy and messed up their lives.

I found my passion in the real estate business. It was exciting and rewarding. I always had a firecracker in my gut that said go for it now and do more and then do more again. I liked to stay busy. Fancy houses and fancy cars definitely didn't drive me, not at all. A lot of my friends went out and bought everything they could get their hands on—new houses, new cars, all the jewelry they could buy, and lots of fancy clothes. The exception was one of my dear friends who is still my very best friend today, Alberta. She was like me—way more conservative and always planning for the future for her children and her.

Alberta was raising her two kids by herself and also had been poor as a child. Needless to say we are the only ones who are financially OK today. When I was a real estate agent, I still drove my ten-year-old Ford and moved from house to house fixing them up. I was selling them and going on to the next thing to start over again. Brad and I lived in a few of them but not for long. Thank God—they were not pleasant to live in while we were fixing them up.

I was always driven to create something good for myself and for everyone else around me. I didn't need power or wealth for any reason except to take the fear out of my gut about making it on my own. I had to know I could take care of my son and me. I was a project person with a fire in my gut to perform. It was so much fun, but it became very addictive, much like it affects any other workaholic.

There were a lot of things to put together to make it work out. My clients had a lot of questions. I found out I loved to solve problems for people. That's why the real estate business worked for me. I liked helping people pick out the houses that would suit them best. I felt like a counselor half the time, and I had my own clients.

There was the screening of what they wanted. Then there was the sale of their home, and then we had to find them another home in the right neighborhood. Then I had to find the right financing that would work for them. This was all in a short amount of time.

It was challenging, but I loved it, which meant a lot of paperwork and computer work. I felt a great reward and felt successful when I was done. I even got paid for having all that fun. Then I had to start all over and do it again and again. I had to love it. I knew people born poor like me would be the only ones who would do all that work. Because this job was 24/7 and then some, I had to love serving and helping all the people with their personal needs. Buying property was the biggest decision they were ever going to make in their lives. They needed some guidance along the way, not to make a decision for them but to be there for whatever questions they might have and to ease their minds.

I always lived within my means. I put 90 percent back into my investments, looking to the future, and it worked out. You have to have patience and a goal, and believe you can have it.

CHAPTER 28

Philippines

I TOOK A pilgrim trip to the Philippines and saw all different kinds of religions. I went with a church group from my neighborhood. I got to see how they did their worshiping and healing. We stayed in a nice motel to start, but as we got more into the country things got a little rough. They had a paper shortage most of the time we were there so we had to pay two dollars for one square of toilet paper, and you couldn't get more than four at a time. And that's if we were in a place where we could even get some!

Our trip was mapped out for us, and we had a guide. I would say, never go without one. He knew the lingo and where it was safe and where it was not.

It was still rough for us sometimes. Other countries are not like ours. There was no law of protection. Just about anything goes. Mostly it was about who had the money and how they were going to get it from us. Maybe they would do something peaceful or maybe they would just steal it. We never knew.

Remember, these people were pretty desperate. Most of their needs were not met at any time. I'm talking about general needs such as food and medicine or staying warm or cool.

Our church had been there many times, so we were told it would be OK. We got to see the different ways they thought about God. It was not at all the way we thought about God. The whole trip was inspiring and spiritual, and I definitely felt closer to God when we were done. We went for two weeks, and we were always traveling while we were there. I can't tell you all the places we went.

I was really in culture shock. All Americans should take a trip to a third-world country. Then they would take care of, protect, and appreciate their county a lot more.

I had never seen so many people living in cardboard boxes. The boxes were attached to each other so they could hold each other up. There were no bathrooms, no water, no showers, and I definitely felt guilty for having meat on my bones. It's a sight to see, and you will never forget it.

What a great trip, and it was educational. After three weeks, I went back to Sacramento and continued to work in the church. I really enjoyed it. It was volunteer work, and that's what made it so special. I was still working my real estate business at that time, and it took care of my son and me financially. It seemed like the closer I got to God, the more he would take care of me, and I had a lot more joy, forgiveness, and love in my heart.

They took another trip to the Philippines about two years later, and I went along. It was so great the first time that I wanted to feel that good again. I felt enlightened. The second time was even better because I could understand things a little better.

When you take a trip like that, you are thinking of nothing except God and connecting to your source. You feel like you get a renewal of God's acceptance of you—the person he created in perfect form.

When I got home the real estate market was falling apart and, I certainly didn't want to live through that again. It had been hard the first time around. I found out the real estate market was an up-and-down business. I knew I needed something more stable.

Brad said he wanted to move to Oregon. I thought the timing was good and it was a good idea. I didn't want to hang around Sacramento for another five years of hard times. That's how long I knew it might take for the market to turn around.

So we decided to move to Oregon. It was time to move on to the next adventure in life. I believed I had a passion for everything I did, and I was lucky because I loved all my jobs. If I didn't, I would not waste my time. I would move on.

CHAPTER 29

My Motivation Started When I Was a Child

ALWAYS SAID I wanted to try everything in life. It all looked so exciting. I didn't want to miss anything. But when I look at the overall picture, I'm glad I missed a lot of things.

1. I was the little girl down the street selling lemonade in my front yard.
2. Then I was the neighborhood babysitter.
3. I cleaned houses and yards for people in my neighborhood.
4. I sold Fuller Brush door to door.
5. Then I sold lingerie and had parties in everybody's houses. I had different models in each home. It was a lot of fun. I made good money.
6. Then I tried to work for the phone company, and they said I didn't have a soft voice for the job.
7. I tried to be a waitress and I couldn't cut it—another one down the drain.
8. That's when I found an amusement park at the beach called The Pike in Long Beach, California. I worked very hard, and I had a passion for that job.
9. Then I bought and worked in my two concessions on The Pike.

The Carnival Girl

10. I found the traveling carnival and had a big passion for that. I loved my job, and I loved that I was responsible for people having fun.
11. Then my son Brad and I had a firewood business for about five years.
12. Now there was the trucking business with my boyfriend for four years.
13. Then I became a real estate agent for twelve years.
14. I bought land and a bar in Rio Linda.
15. I bought real estate houses, fixed them up, and then sold them.
16. I bought bare land and became a developer.
17. I bought and sold many of my own commercial real estate investments.
18. I worked in the church for two and a half years.
19. Then I became a minister for another two years. Then we moved to Oregon for five years.
20. Brad and I bought a grocery store.
21. I also bought a commercial building next door.
22. Then Brad and I bought a convenience store with a Texaco gas station. That we owned for about seven years.
23. There were also fifty-four units in the mini-storage I bought and owned for about seven years.
24. I sold health products online for about one year.
25. Now I have three duplexes and three houses as rentals.
26. At the moment, I'm trying to finish this book, which will then make me an author. I would call that finally semi-retired!

CHAPTER 30

Back to My Real Estate Story in Sacramento

I HAD LIVED through one recession in the real estate business in 1982, and I did not want to go through that again. It would have been four or five years of hanging around and having a hard time.

And I didn't like it when I had to sell people homes because times were tough and the economy was bad. It was a sad time for the people who had lost their jobs and were losing their homes. It wasn't fun anymore.

We took the plunge and moved to Oregon. Willie Nelson came to mind again, "On the Road Again." I could never forget him. He was the best, and I loved his song. It has been my life.

I had lived in my new house for about three years, and my son had lived in his for about two years. We had good equity in both of our houses—enough to move to Oregon. So we both sold our houses and had plenty of money for our new plans. We knew we would be able to buy something when we got there. We were looking for a business and a separate home for each of us. We were ready for our new start. My angel said it's time to move on!

I had paid off my house, so I had to refinance it and then pull out most of the money. That way we didn't have to wait for the sale to go through. I had heard I was about the last person to get a loan in the Sacramento area. They had pulled the plug on the Sacramento lending market.

My angels were working hard for me again. My timing was good. I did get out before the recession hit again in 1991. Then I had my friend Alberta put my house on the market to sell. We made it a good price so it would sell right away, and so it did.

We wanted it to go away quickly, and we got lucky. A nice family bought it. They moved in within thirty days, and we closed escrow. They had three horses, and they needed the space for their horses. It was the perfect property for them. It had lots of space, and it was out in the country and private and quiet. Everybody was happy.

And then the state of California charged me a 3 percent tax on top of the sales price because I moved out of state. I think that was a bad law the state made. They were ripping me off, and it was legal. And they did the same to my son. It wasn't right that they had a license to steal. That was our money, not theirs. We earned it, they didn't. They made a lot more money than we did, but they still had to take ours. My real signal was when everything went together smoothly.

We knew this was a good time to go for it. Our new adventure was coming right up!

CHAPTER 31

When We First Arrived in Oregon

BRAD RAN INTO a friend from Sacramento named Eddie. It was quite a surprise and a good one. Eddie was getting ready to go to a real, live roundup in Ola, Idaho, close to Boise.

Eddie invited us to the roundup and asked Brad if he would like to be part of it. We were excited because we had never even seen a real roundup—and then to be asked to be part of it! How exciting for Brad.

We took off and drove over to Ola and got a motel room in Emit, which was next to Ola. When we got up the next morning, we went for a little breakfast in one of the local restaurants. The restaurant was cute as a bug, with real country food. There were nothing but cowboys in that restaurant. In a sense, we were having our breakfast with real cowboys. How exciting! We loved it and wished we could stay in that town, but there was no way to make a living there, so we had to move on.

The next day we got to live the cowboy dream of being part of a real, live roundup. Brad would finally be part of the Old West, even though it was just for one day. It was exciting to be part of the whole experience.

Brad liked it so much in Emmett that he went back a year later to participate with the Indians and celebrate the Fourth of July with them. Brad even brought Cheryl, his new girlfriend, with him, and they said they really had a great time.

Brad and I had decided to be partners again, which always worked out well for us. We went looking for a new business, hoping to buy a grocery store. We were looking for a new life. We looked for something for about four months before we found what we wanted. Brad had always wanted to move to Oregon where there was good hunting and fishing, so his dream was coming true. I love it when your dreams come true, don't you?

We looked at a lot of grocery stores once we got into Oregon, from southern Oregon to the middle of the state. Brad had always wanted a grocery store. He had a lot of experience from when he had worked with his Uncle Paul in Lake Tahoe, Nevada. I had the business experience, so we figured we would be a good team. I said, "Let's go for it. I'm sure we can do this." We were a little scared because we had never done anything like that before—but I had always said, "No guts, no glory."

We found a seller who had seven stores scattered all over the state, so we looked at all the numbers and all the stores. This took us about four months, traveling all over the state. We settled in Springfield, across the bridge from Eugene, which was a college town. A lot of the college kids lived in Springfield because it was a lot cheaper for them. All the rentals were about half the price of housing in Eugene, and the food was a lot cheaper for them. You would have thought we were in another state instead of right across the bridge.

Springfield's prices were so different. We did very well and had a good time with our new grocery-store business. It was a neighborhood store, so we put a big table and lots of chairs right in the middle of the store, and we became the hang out. You could play Keno all day in Oregon.

We always had a tableful, especially in the morning when they would come in and have their coffee and doughnuts and play a little Keno. With lots of people hanging out at our store, we were pretty safe, even though working in a mom-and-pop grocery store had been rated as the second most unsafe job in America. But we

When We First Arrived in Oregon

knew we had to buy a job, so this was the one. Now, a grocery store was something we thought we could do. It worked out fine because, again, we always had our angels with us, taking care of us.

We had pull-tab tickets so players didn't have to go far to gamble all day. Keno and pull tabs were on the menu every day—breakfast, lunch, and dinner and play your favorite game at your local grocery store. "Buy and play at Horne's Market" was the buzz around town. It was a lot of fun for gamblers in our neighborhood.

Oregon was something else. After we had been there almost a year, we knew most of our customers and had a real nice clientele built up.

Next, my Uncle Russ, Ronnie, and I decided to sell our twenty acres in Cave Junction, Oregon. It was a beautiful piece of property. We tried to vacation there once a year. We had lots of good family barbecues and lots of swimming in the river. It lasted for about five years. It was really hard to sell that property, because we had really enjoyed it, but we got too busy to go there, so it was time. It was a beautiful property, and we owned land on both sides of the river, which meant we could build a house on either side.

We found out some other people from the mountain were occupying our property. They were bad drug addicts. We put it on the market and sold it to a doctor in California. Unfortunately, we still had the problem with the dopers on the mountain. So Brad went to scare them off. He took his .45-caliber gun with him. He didn't see anyone when he got there. They had disappeared, but they knew Brad was in town for sure.

It was still a very small town. When you walked into the grocery store, everybody who lived in the area knew you were there.

Brad went to the property again and could not find anyone. He decided to leave them a message, so he shot a lot of bullets in the air while he was there. Then he went back to the local grocery store and told the clerk we had sold the property and that somebody with a lot of money would be up in a week to claim it. Brad said the dopers needed to clear out their stuff within a week, before the doctor got there, or he would have to come back with his friends and clear it out for them.

"I don't think they want me to do that, because there wouldn't be anything left when I'm done with everything," Brad told him. "We told the buyer it should be cleared out by the time he gets there, and if it isn't he can call us, and we will come and clear everything out, trucks and all."

We never heard from the doctor, so we figure either he took care of everything himself or everything went OK.

Now we were all back in Springfield, and within a year I had bought the building next to our grocery store. I paid it off within the next two years. I rented it out to the Goodwill Company in Springfield. That was for four years, and they were the best tenants I ever had. They did their own repairs and paid right on time every month.

I bought a piece of land and had a duplex built for me. It was nice to be able to pick out what I wanted for the home where I was going to be living. It was almost walking distance to the store. I really liked that.

CHAPTER 32

Brazil

I HEARD MY church in California was going to Brazil, so I said, "Brazil, here I come!" I had always wanted to go to Brazil, and going with the church would be lots of fun.

It was 1994, and we had been in Oregon for about three years. I excitedly flew back to Sacramento and saw my old friends. We left right after I arrived. We were on our way to Brazil.

We went for three weeks. It was a long ride in the plane, but they showed us some good movies that helped make the trip seem a lot shorter. That definitely made it more interesting and took my mind off being in the plane for so long. We always went in a group which was nice. We had a guide, and we had our trip well planned out before we went. We were in Rio de Janeiro for the New Year's Eve party. What a sight to see! All I could say was, "Unbelievable!"

The natives were all wearing white and lining up on the beach for their healing from the gods, drinking their booze straight and smoking their cigars. They said they were calling in the different kinds of spirits to do the healing. These transmediums, as they were called, were jumping up and down and all around, singing, smoking their cigars, and drinking their whiskey.

They said drinking the booze and smoking the cigars with the dancing and singing was going to help the other healing spirits come into their body and allow the ones in there to take a hike for a while. It was interesting to see the different cultures and how everybody believed. There are so many different ways people worship in our world.

From traveling around in one country, I was certainly getting an education on how many different religions there are and how differently people worship. I don't know how many different ways of worshipping there are. But in Brazil I can see many. I now can see that none of them are alike.

The beaches in Brazil were beautiful, pure, white sand, and they kept them very clean. We did see the topless bathing suits in the daytime on the beach. The guys were having a great time walking around. They were definitely different from our beaches at home. Most of the Brazilian people didn't think much of it. But we were from America, and we didn't want to participate in their customs. We had no volunteers in our group!

The one and only Amazon Jungle Tower Hotel and tightrope walking bridge in Brazil.

Brazil

While we were in Brazil, we took off and landed twenty-eight times in three weeks. I never wanted to see another airplane in my life. Our feet were swelling from going up and down so much. Brazil is big, and the things we wanted to see were all spread out. We, of course, wanted to see the different religions and how they worshiped their gods. We saw them worship aliens and animals from the sea, plus a bit of voodoo, and there were psychic healers too. We went along with the ceremonies to see what they were about.

One of the best ones I remember was the German camp. They had many bungalows, and they took care of the old and the very young. It was supported by donations from the Germans who used to live in Germany but had moved to Brazil. They lived in Germany during the war. It was like they were trying to give back something of what they had taken away at one time or another. Old and sick Germans were running the place. They made no profit on the business because it was all goodwill.

This was a sight to see. There was one building they had boarded up and said they couldn't use. The guide told us when the people had first come from Germany, the building was used for human experiments. That was a little creepy—it was really hard to hear about those kinds of things. It seemed so inhumane and, of course, it was.

This is a monkey's life at the Amazon Jungle Tower Hotel in Brazil. Looks like it's an adventurous life for the monkeys!

The Carnival Girl

The Germans made us a nice lunch, and we joined with the people who lived there to enjoy the meal. They talked about how they didn't have enough room for everybody because the need was becoming larger all the time. When we mentioned the empty building, we thought they were going to have a collective heart attack. We had forgotten about that situation. One of the guides had told us earlier that was used for experiment in the early days. They just looked at us and then said we never use that boarded up building. Then they acted like we never had said anything about the building. They just changed the subject.

Phyllis relaxing at the Amazon River in Brazil.

They had their own garden, and the food was good and fresh. They told us a story about the land's condition when they first had moved there and how they had improved it and made a real nice place to live for all their people. They were so far away from any town, you would have thought they were living in a world by themselves.

There were a lot of cities like that in Brazil. The government left them alone and didn't stop people from gathering away by themselves. They were allowed to live their own lifestyle.

At one of the camps, we saw them dance and sing to the alien beings and ask for healings for the sick. They didn't have too many doctors around, but they had their herbs and prayers. I believe their average lifespan was forty to fifty years old, so with our visit I guess they were looking at some of the oldest people they had ever seen.

When we were at the voodoo camp, they were definitely strange. They danced and sang to the spirit and acted like they were a little crazy. We were told they left their bodies, and other spirits came in to heal their bodies. We were also told that they weren't doing their real ceremonies in front of us.

It was a great trip, and we had a lot of fun. The American government would put a stop to that kind of living. They would stop you because they now want to control everything you do.

We next went to the Amazon and down the river in a big boat to the only motel in the jungle. How exciting!

As we were coming off the boat, the people who ran the motel greeted us nicely. Then we were greeted again by the monkeys. As they walked up to us, they put a tropical drink right in our hands. They were well-trained, and they looked so cute. Later on, they tried to steal everything we had. For instance, I had a camera in my hand, and one of the monkeys grabbed for it. I pulled it away, and then he put his tail around my neck and swung around to reach for my camera. By now he was choking me, so I started screaming. The manager from the motel came running out and talked to the monkey in some kind of lingo. The monkey heard him and stopped. That was quite interesting and a little scary to see who was really in charge.

Our rooms didn't have enclosed ceilings on them. It was very hot so they needed circulation.

The monkeys would go into our rooms and help themselves to what they wanted, mostly when we were not there. But sometimes when we were there, we had to chase them away. If they saw us coming, they would go away until we were gone and then come back to our room again. They definitely were trained for the job—there were no dummies in this jungle. Luckily we had a good attitude about the whole thing.

This was the end of our trip, and we needed some R & R. It had been a lot of traveling in a three-week period, and we desperately needed our rest. They said you could get tried just from all the ups and downs. But we never stopped for a minute, because we wanted to see as much as we could.

It was beautiful at the resort, and they had a lot of great food suited for people from other countries. We could not eat their native food. They have different diseases, so if we had eaten their native food, it would have been at our own risk. Some of the young girls with us ate their fish, and they got very sick.

The rooms in Brazil were quite a treat. You had to walk on a tightrope to get to your room. It was like the Tarzan movies, but now I was living it. Oh, boy, what fun that was! The rope walkways were used to get you to your rooms, which were not attached to the dining and entertainment areas. That's how we traveled from place to place. They were made to take you all over the motel and to the different rows of rooms. The idea was to keep you high up in the air and to keep the animals away so you could walk around freely.

We loved to eat on the patio outside the restaurant where it was beautiful and safe. The patio was high up in the air; only the monkeys could get to us. We did see a bobcat walking down below us one day. But we weren't bothered by it. It was quite interesting to see. We had a nice breeze blowing through the motel. It was about eighty degrees there in the middle of the jungle. I understand it gets pretty hot in town, though—like about 110 degrees.

Saturday and Sunday was the end of our three-week stay. By then the need for rest and relaxation had kicked in and we were ready to go home. Three weeks away from home is a long time—we were getting homesick.

I didn't know the jungle was such a beautiful place. The air was fresh, and the wild jungle had a romantic side to it. It made you feel as though you had gone back in time to a different world where life was free and simple, like in the old-time pictures of my grandpa and grandma. I think there is a little yearning in all of us to go back to when it was simple.

Again, we were on the walkway going from one cabin to another. We were safe from all the animals except the monkeys, which I didn't think were so cute anymore. They were wild animals, and they were way stronger then we were. When they wanted something from you, you might as well give it to them, because you couldn't win.

Some in our group went alligator hunting at night, which meant getting into the boat and catching the alligators. They were baby alligators, but one night the boat tipped over and they had to rush to get back into the boat before one of the alligators bit them. That is one activity I chose not to do; it was a little dangerous. I wasn't into danger. We saw those little tars—piranhas in the water—but those darling fish could eat you alive in about three seconds. We could see them from the small boat in which we were traveling around the jungle—a little scary!

Going to Brazil was the best present I ever could have given myself. I learned and lived at least three different lifetimes with my experiences in one trip to Brazil versus just remaining in the real world.

There were a lot of poor people in Brazil, like the Philippines. They lived in cardboard houses leaning against each other. It was a sad thing to see.

We should never complain in the U.S. There are only two classes of people in third-world counties. In Brazil when they say "the rich" and "the poor," they mean just that. There is no in-between. It's a hard life. Since their life span on an average is forty to fifty years old, everybody is young, which means that very young people are running that country. Many of the people there were far from any clean water and had no real bathrooms. Sometimes they would have to walk a mile or two to get one bucket of water.

A few months after we arrived home, I got really sick with malaria. None of the doctors in Oregon knew what was wrong with me. I almost died.

It was summertime, and I was very dehydrated. Finally, the bank teller where I banked realized they hadn't seen me at the bank for three days. She knew I should have been coming into the bank every day to make my deposits, and she knew Brad was out of town hunting. It was a small town, so they knew our habits. So they sent a scout to check on me. I had a high fever and couldn't get out of the bed. They took me to the hospital.

The doctor tried to handle the fever, because he didn't know what else to do. They wanted to do exploratory surgery in my stomach and I said, "No, thanks." I believed it had nothing to do with my stomach.

The symptoms returned the next summer, but they weren't so strong. I was ready for it this time. I figured I knew what I had to do. So I bought a lot of aspirin to keep the fever down, and I stocked up on lots of liquids. This time I didn't go to the doctor. I kept drinking lots of water and juices, and I stayed in bed and waited it out. In two weeks I was OK.

When we came home, we had learned to appreciate running water, electricity, paved roads, real bathrooms, our nice parks, our great highways, and much more.

Everyone who hates to pay his or her taxes should take a trip to a third-world country. Not to say everything is always OK in America, but what we have is so much better then anywhere else. As long as they don't raise our taxes too much, and we can keep working and have some entertainment in our lives, we should stay pretty happy and feel very lucky.

Make sure whomever you vote for doesn't want to be like those other countries. We don't want to be anything like them. Too much government will do that to our country in the long run. So stand up and don't let it happen. Remember: "For the people and by the people."

CHAPTER 33

Saving the Owl, Starving the People

WHEN I GOT home, I heard President Clinton and Al Gore had decided to save the owls in the forest. Oregon business went down the tubes. Oregonians lived off the forestland, and now it was closed—no logging, no forest work of any kind. All of these companies were closed throughout the whole state. Montana, Wyoming, and other states had areas for the spotted owl and other animals the environmentalists wanted to save over and above the human race.

Oregon went into a deep depression. People lost their homes, and they stood in lines at the food bank for the first time in their lives. They got divorced, and some moved away. The people who made the decision to save the spotted owl created a recession in Oregon and other areas while they were still flying around in their jets. They were still going on their great vacations and having great holidays and living it up. They were not hungry, losing their homes, or standing in lines at the food bank. The bottom line was, the government did not care about the hardships they were imposing on the Oregon people and the other states where they had shut down forest work.

This was a big lesson for me that the government could allow people to go hungry and lose everything they owned. They certainly were not living the same life the Oregonians were living. That was the worst decision I saw the environmentalists make.

Our business was in trouble like many others. We started looking again to figure out where to go next. All of Oregon was depressed, and we didn't know when it was going to get better. I always felt like there was a higher power controlling things for us. And I was getting the message to move on.

It was time to make a move again to Idaho or Montana. Hello, Willie Nelson: "On the road again." We decided to check out Idaho and Montana, where the economy would be better. We had heard there was a lot more money in those parts and a lot of different enterprising businesses to pursue.

First, I took a trip with a friend around only the northern parts of both states. I was checking out what the states looked like and how it felt to be there. Brad and I had decided to pick Idaho because that state seemed to have a lot more small businesses from which to choose.

The next time I went to look around again, I went by myself, and I drove all over before I ended up in Sandpoint, Idaho, real close to Canada. It was beautiful country there.

I found a mini-storage in Sandpoint that was in my budget, so I went ahead and bought the mini-storage. There were fifty-four units and an extra big lot so you could expand if you wanted. There was room to put about fifty-four more units on the property. I put a good down payment on it, and within two years I had paid it off completely.

At the same time we were still maintaining our grocery-store business in Oregon. We worked it ourselves—it was a real mom-and-pop operation. My duplex was paid for so there was no money going out there, and we didn't have to pay for any babysitters. We took the kids with us to work or whoever was off for the day was the babysitter. But business had slowed down a lot. It wasn't easy for two families to live off of that income, but we did. We did without a lot of things we wanted and only bought what we needed. It was sad to see the nice people in our little neighborhood suffering and going downhill.

Saving the Owl, Starving the People

Everybody started drinking more—and those were our best sales yet. It was not a fun time to watch the destruction going on with our sweet little neighborhood. The government had turned everything around in Oregon, and there was more unhappiness than I ever wanted to see. From now on I will be watching everything the government does and I will be participating in making it turn out the right way—as the Constitution states, "For the people and by the people." I will be watching the Republican party and the Democratic party closely.

The kids liked hanging out in the store with us. Or maybe we should call it playing in the store. After the first year, Brad and his wife split up, and she took the kids back to California. Brad and I thought we were going to die. Nobody knew she was going to be leaving. She just took off one afternoon while we were working. It didn't take long—about three days—before the kids called and said, "Daddy, please come and get us." They were not happy there.

She didn't have permission to take them out of state. Brad had to make two trips to get them. His wife talked little Erica into staying when Brad went down the first time. He came back with his son, Brian, and we were so happy to have him back home again but sad Erica didn't come home with her brother. A few days later, little Erica called again and said, "Daddy, please come and get me. I really want to come home and live with you." Brad made his second trip to pick up Erica, and he had his family back. He was real happy about how it turned out.

I was glad my grandkids were coming home. I couldn't think about living life without them. And we never heard from Brad's wife again as long as we lived in Oregon. She had a drug problem. I was sad for her, but Brad and I tried to help her and we couldn't. She wasn't a bad person, she just had a problem we couldn't help her with.

After living in Idaho for four years, Erica called her mom and asked her to come to Idaho and visit them. The good news was she said she was clean, she was glad to get the call, and she would love to come and visit. The kids were happy—losing her had left an empty spot in their lives. One of the reasons we had moved away from California was we were trying to change her surroundings and get her clean. But it didn't happen at that time. As the saying goes, you can't do it for them—they have to do it for themselves.

Brad had to raise his children by himself, but of course I took the other half of the job. It wasn't hard to help take care of my grandchildren. I loved them like my own. They were my life, and I wanted to take care of them and enjoy their love. Children always have a lot of love to give.

We can learn a lot from our children and grandchildren. They know the real stuff about life we sometimes have forgotten—such as what really makes the world go around is lots of love.

Things still were not going too good for us in Oregon, and we were getting ready to move on. Brad and I talked about being ready to hit the road again and find a better place to live. The next day, we put the store on the market and were ready to go.

We sold our store in Oregon right away to a Korean family. They were moving into the area. The timing was good, and we needed to go see what we could find in Idaho to buy. First, I went to look around again in Sandpoint where I already had my mini-storage units. I stayed for three days, but the real estate agents couldn't find anything for me. I went back home and told Brad it was his turn. I watched the store that time so Brad and his girlfriend, Cheryl, could go looking the next day in Idaho.

Brad went to Coeur d'Alene, Idaho, right across from Spokane, Washington, and he liked the area a lot. He stayed for a week, looking at the different businesses to buy, until he found a small mom-and-pop store. It was a Shell gas station and convenience store on a business street in downtown Coeur d'Alene.

He hadn't seen the store yet, but he had the owner's name and number. They owned many other big gas stations in town. As he was leaving town, Brad met one of the owners who had the main big gas station and convenience store in town.

The owner told Brad where the store was located, so when he got back home to Oregon he told me about it. He gave me the owner's name and number. He told me it sounded pretty good and I should go check it out.

Saving the Owl, Starving the People

The next day I went to Coeur d'Alene to check it out. I somehow lost the paper Brad had given me with the name and number on it. I was pretty upset with myself because I had come all that way. So there was no way I was going home empty-handed.

I got a telephone book and said to myself, *Well, you're going to call every gas station in the book until you find the owner who wants to sell his mom-and-pop gas station.* I opened the telephone book and found the pages where the gas station and convenience stores were and I said, "Here goes." I started calling and asking for the owners and if they had a small mom-and-pop gas station for sale.

After the first hour of calling I found the one who had a mom-and-pop gas station and convenience store for sale. I didn't know if it was the same one my son had found, but at this point it didn't matter.

There were my angels again. When it goes together real easy, that means the right thing is happing right then. The owner invited me to his place of business, and I said I'd be right over. It was the weekend, so I went right over and met the owner at his place. Then I asked to look at the books and told him he was asking too much for what the net was on the books.

"Phyllis, go and write me your best offer on a sheet of paper," he said.

I went to the store and bought a yellow notebook tablet. Then I proceeded to write him my best offer and took it back to him the same day. He said yes. I certainly was a little surprised, because it was a lot cheaper then he had said he had wanted. Later on I heard he had bought two different gas stations—one small and one big—but he only wanted the big one. My timing was good because he really didn't even want the mom-and-pop store; he wanted to get rid of it.

We made a deal right then and there on a piece of notebook paper. It was a one-page contract and reminded me of the good old days—like a handshake or a contract on a plain sheet of paper. I loved it. We didn't have to go back and forth. I do remember when things were done like that. I had to find a good ol' boy in Idaho for it to happen again.

The Carnival Girl

I went back to Oregon and told Brad to start packing, that we had bought a convenience store and gas station. We had only thirty days until escrow would close. I had sold my duplex and my commercial building. The only thing we had left to sell was Brad's house, and we were going to let the real estate agent sell it after we left. It worked out well. Our store in Oregon would close escrow about ten days before the one in Idaho would close.

We had to say goodbye to our friends in Oregon. It was a sad thing to do. We had thought Oregon was going to be our home forever. We were getting settled in real good. The first three years, we didn't even see much rain. But the last year two years were wet and rainy, so it really made it easier to get out of Oregon. All that rain is what we heard was normal.

Then we got a phone call from the buyer for the Oregon store. He called to say they couldn't get the money they were planning on, so they would have to cancel their transaction.

"Brad, we're going to move to Idaho anyway," I said. "You and your Cheryl and her three children and your son, Brian, should go as planned, leaving five days from now."

Erica, my granddaughter, wanted to stay with me, so I was happy about that.

About six months later Erica wanted to join her dad in Idaho, so I took her to the airport and said my goodbyes. I knew I was going to miss her a lot. Erica and Brian were like my second kids.

I went to the bank and borrowed some money so we could continue to purchase the store in Idaho. We didn't want to lose that store. It was a very good deal for us and what we wanted. I couldn't get enough money from the bank so I borrowed it from my credit cards, which sounds insane, but we had no choice. We still needed about eighty thousand dollars to close escrow in Idaho.

We were playing a long shot on our future, but we had no other choice. I was working on faith again from my angels. They had always steered me right.

I would stay in Oregon until the next summer and put the store back on the market. Things in that area sold only in the summer, unlike California.

Saving the Owl, Starving the People

The time passed very fast. I called my brother and my mom and asked them to come visit me. I asked them to stay for a while to help me out.

My brother said, "Phyllis, I'll come in one week. I'm finishing up a job, and the next one doesn't come up for another month."

I was excited my brother was coming. I hadn't seen him for a long time. He was back in Santa Rosa, California, on his friend's property, living in a bus he had converted into a home. He was still my hippie brother, but our love had never changed, even though we lived completely different lives. By then he had given up his extra activities and only drank alcohol here and there.

I knew he was going to be a big help to me. I needed all the help I could get. My mom said she'd also hang out and help me out for a while. When they arrived in Springfield, I was living in Brad's house. I was remodeling it and getting it ready to sell, so I asked my brother to stay with me for a year to help me run the store and do the remodel. Again, I got lucky, and he said yes. He said the job he had coming up wasn't important to him. I had a lot on my plate and was happy to have the help. I really needed him.

Ronnie and my mom were my angels. There are a lot of angels in this world. You have to look for them, but you will find them everywhere. My niece, Angie, came to Oregon for a short time and helped me out. But things came up for her, and she had to go back to California.

Brad had to start from scratch. For the first time, he was going to have to do everything himself to get the business going. He never had taken care of the business side of things before.

One day he called me and said, "Mom, I'm doing fine. The title company and the city of Coeur d'Alene are helping me on what step to take next and which license to apply for."

"Brad, I knew you could do it, and I'm real proud of you," I said. "There is a lot to do before you can ever open the doors to any business."

"Mom, I went a little crazy, but I got it going, and we are open for business."

Brad ran the complete business for one full year before I could join him in Idaho. It took me that year to sell the store in Oregon. We sold Brad's house for him before we left Oregon—to another Korean family. There were a lot of Korean families moving to Oregon. They were building new plants for the latest computer parts. I guess that was their specialty. We were glad to see them coming into the area and buying the store and the house.

We left Oregon when our business was complete. In July 1997, my brother, my mom, and I took off for Idaho, singing our favorite song, "On the Road Again."

Saving the Owl, Starving the People

A picture of our grocery store that my son and
I owned in Springfield, Oregon, in 1994.

My son, brother, and I working in our grocery store in Springfield,
Oregon, in 1995.

CHAPTER 84

Moving to Idaho, Our Last Frontier

WE ARRIVED IN Coeur d'Alene, Idaho, in July 1997. It was a beautiful day with the sun streaming down on us, and we were looking at a nice blue sky. We had happiness in our hearts and souls. We were so excited to finely be in Idaho, meeting with our family, and knowing we didn't have to go back to Oregon. We were actually there to stay.

Brad and Cheryl were renting a five-bedroom house in Hayden, next to Coeur d'Alene and within five miles of downtown.

We didn't have any extra money, so we moved in with Brad and Cheryl. It was crowded, but we managed for about three months. When I sold the Oregon store, I had to pay back the money I had borrowed to buy the Texaco gas station and convenience store in Idaho. That left Brad and me ten thousand dollars each to purchase a home for ourselves. We finally found two nice houses, only four blocks apart, which made it nice for the kids. They could walk back and forth from house to house. Also the high school was right across the street, which was convenient.

We had just arrived in Idaho, and it wasn't easy. We had to find two different sellers who would carry a loan for us. We didn't have any credit or a two-year income record in the state of Idaho—what the bank wanted before we could qualify for a loan. Again, our angels were with us.

The Carnival Girl

This time it was the gas station business that was different from anything we had ever tried. It was definitely the big boy's game. You needed a lot of money on hand at all times. Every time there was a gas war, we had to pay upfront until the gas war was over. We're talking a lot of cash because that's the only way you could buy your gas. Our gas tanks were pretty big, so we are talking about four thousand to six thousand dollars in cash we had to keep on hand to purchase our gas.

The inside of the convenience store is where we made our money. We only made one to three cents on gas sales.

When the gas war was going on, we sold our gas for less then we bought it for. This was pretty tough. The owners of the gas companies would pay us back for the difference within about three months. That was a long haul for us little mom-and-pop stores. It was a tough game we were playing.

My bookkeeper was having a breakdown every time I used my credit cards to finance these difficult times in the gas-station business. I had to use them again and again to keep things going in the business. This was a big-boy club, and we were right in the middle of it. We knew we had to put our time in and were hoping soon we could sell and get into something else a little easier.

I didn't have any choice. I had good credit with my credit cards, and we needed the money. Again, they bailed us out. Of course our angels were with us, and that's how we made it though the hard times in this gas and convenience-store business. We loved meeting and visiting with all the people. Brad made a lot of hunting and fishing friends, which was, of course, number one on his agenda. That's the reason he wanted to move to Oregon and then Idaho.

I love the weather in Idaho a lot better than Oregon. We have a lot more sunshine here, even when it snows. We love the snow. It is different for us and makes everything in the surrounding area beautiful. We owned and operated the Texaco station from 1996 to 2003, a total of seven years. We certainly learned a lot about big business—meaning the gas business. We really didn't care for it.

Moving to Idaho, Our Last Frontier

Brad and I in front of our Texaco gas and convenience store in
Coeur d'Alene, Idaho, in 1998.

The Carnival Girl

Son Brad and grandson Brian in front of our Texaco convenience store and gas station in Coeur d'Alene, Idaho, in 1999.

Moving to Idaho, Our Last Frontier

My grandson Brian standing in front of our
Texaco gas station in Coeur d'Alene, Idaho, in the year 2000.

The Carnival Girl

Brad, Cheryl, and Michael working in the Texaco station in 2003.

Sammie and I working in the Texaco station in 2003.

Brad, Cheryl, Ronnie, Sammie, and I all worked the store, but we still had to hire other people. We stayed open many hours, from six a.m. until midnight or two a.m.

I enjoyed the people in Idaho. They reminded me of when I lived in Oklahoma and Kansas as a child—good down-to-earth kinds of people. We did have lots of ups and downs in the gas business. The day the motel next door burned down was a very big, scary event. After all, we had gas right next door! The firefighters did a great job of putting out the fire before it got to us—thank God!

We were only robbed two times, and nobody got hurt. They didn't get much money. We did have surveillance tapes, and that helped a lot. Not even our staff could get away with a lot. I remember very clearly the morning I walked into the store, and one of our employees said, "Phyllis, stop and look at the TV." All I could think was, *What are you doing with a TV in the store?* I got upset and couldn't hear anything she was saying to me about the airplane crashing into World Trade Center in New York City.

Evidently someone had brought the TV to the store so we would know what was going on. As I began to wake up, I couldn't believe my eyes. We watched the whole thing on TV. It was like we were in a different world, not the one I know. That day is when America cried—September 11, 2001. We knew life as we knew it would never be the same.

Then, we were just doing business as normal, and here came another tough economy. The buyers from California were coming to Idaho. It always hit them first. By 2003 we had three different people fighting over our store, and we didn't even have it on the market. We know that was a sign that it was time, so we accepted one of the offers and that retired us from the Texaco gas-station business. But we had always known we would need to sell within seven to ten years, because the crime was getting worse. We knew that was the plan before we ever bought our store. So again, our angels were looking out for us.

Brad went on to create his own landscaping business for himself, in Coeur d'Alene, Idaho. Now he lives on a ranch with his wife, Cheryl, on twenty acres that has a creek running through it. Brad loves Idaho; he says Idaho is a good life. I say I agree with him. As a mother, I am very proud of my son. He has created a good life for himself.

I have bought rentals with my half of the sale from the store. So I would say I was semi-retired. That's where we really made our money—from the sale of the real estate.

The first year of being retired in Idaho, I was a lost puppy because I had worked since I was fourteen years old. That's fifty-six years ago! Wow, time flies when you're having fun. After about a year, I bought my rentals, and things started to go real good for me. I was definitely enjoying my retirement. The truth is, before you know it you're retired. Then you have to start up your life all over again because nothing is the same. I went out and joined everything I could and became very busy again. Then my life felt normal. I decided to take a trip to Alaska. So I signed with Holland America for a seven-day cruise, which was just a blast.

Then I got a phone call that my sweet uncle was very sick and might not be living much longer. My mom, my son, and I drove down to Sacramento to visit my Uncle Russ. When we got there, they said he was dying and would be gone in six months. That was breaking our hearts, so we decided to rent a motor home and take him to Oregon to a naturopathic doctor we knew. He said to put him in the hospital, that he needed some blood. They gave him two pints of blood right away. Uncle Russ's brain started working again as best as it could.

They were going to let him die in Sacramento. The Oregon hospital had saved his life. It was the weekend, so there was no communication with the computers in Sacramento until Monday. When Monday came, they said his doctor in Sacramento had told him to go home because they would not be treating him for anything else. I wanted to take him home with me, but his wife said he should come home, and so he wanted to go home. I begged him to come home with me so I could take care of him, but he had already forgotten how he was treated at home. I told Uncle Russ they were going to let him die and his wife wouldn't be helping him out one bit. Sadly, that is what happened.

My mom stayed in Sacramento to help take care of him, but after a while his wife wouldn't let her come over. The wife said she just wanted it to be over. Sadly, my Uncle Russ was eighty-three when he passed.

Within two years I got that same phone call again. It was from my sister. Mom had had a five-way bypass on her heart. The next morning, Ronnie and I flew down to see Mom. Ronnie stayed about two weeks, and I stayed for thirty days. They put Mom into a nursing home so she could finish recuperating, so my sister and I stayed with her all day, every day. It wasn't a nice place to be—matter of fact, it was awful and not clean.

Finally we got her home. I returned home to Idaho, thinking everything was OK, but within a week she was back in the hospital with pneumonia. Within a couple of days, she had passed away from pneumonia.

My mom was eighty-five when she passed. I think it was about a year before I become normal again. I sat at home and did nothing. I don't care what anybody says, you never get over their being gone. I miss them so much—as much today as I did three or five years ago. It's not any easier. That leaves me to be the eldest in the family, and I never thought I would be.

I was angry and sad that I hadn't been able to save either one of them. They were important to me, and I couldn't help them.

Then my brother got sick. First he had a heart attack. Then two years later he got cancer. We went to Mexico for treatments, and soon he was going on six years without cancer. We did come back to the U.S. to have his surgery.

But when he returned from visiting our mom in California, he had a stroke the same time Mom passed away. We didn't want to tell him, but the doctor said he had the right to know then, not later. I didn't want to lose another of my loved ones. But we took the doctor's advice and told our brother. He was unhappy, but he made it through. My brother was a very strong-minded person and I was glad about that.

Please appreciate all your loved ones. They might be gone tomorrow, and you might not get another chance. Sometimes it's

OK not to be right all the time. I'm going to do my best to appreciate everyone and everything in my life like it's my last day on earth. I'm going to thank God every day for all the blessings he has given me and thank him for today! We don't know how long we are going to be here, so I'm certainly going to try to make every day count.

The good news is my seventh great-grandchild was born. How exciting is that? I couldn't wait. Life is feeling good again! Miss Gracie is her name, and she was eight pounds and one ounce, plus twenty inches long. The family was very happy—she is a very beautiful baby. She is perfect, like a miracle from God. But I think all babies are miracles and gifts from God, don't you? The rest of my gifts from God which are the other great-grandchildren. There names are Ashley, Isaiah, Adam, Bella, Ethanie, Tristin, and now Gracie.

Now I'm asking myself, "What's next?" Where will my passion go now? Where will it take me? When I think about the gypsy life I led, it definitely brings a smile to my face. That was a great time in my life. I know my passion right now is to finish this book.

So I'm thinking about sending in my manuscript to my publisher for them to take the next step and send it to the typesetting department. Now it is the first day of January 2011. Margie Miller just called me, so now I am reminded about another lesson. I learned this one from Margie, whom I met in Sacramento. We worked together in a Century 21 real estate office as agents. She is still a very good friend of mine. On New Year's Day every year, the first thing you should do, if possible, is to show up at the door of those you love, or call them, and wish them a happy New Year. The idea is to say hello to all the people who are important to you in your life. Margie would say that's really what it's all about, and the only way to start out your New Year.

Thank you, Margie, for the big reminder and hello I get every year from you, for the last twenty years. I have lots of friends I met in Sacramento, and we have all moved to different areas—Texas, Nevada, Arkansas, Arizona, and me to Idaho. How nice it is that we all stay in touch!

Finishing this book will be one more added adventure to my life. God has given me so many gifts, and now he has made me an author. I do know now I'm going to start saving my money so I can do some traveling overseas and in the U.S.

I believe God wanted me to share my life experience. I'm hoping this book will inspire others to find the gifts God has given them. If you have God as your partner, you will find them all.

Hey, the carnival is in town and the great-grandkids are here now! I have a great idea. Let's go to the carnival!

[Jesus said,] "Everything is possible for one who believes."
—Mark 9:23

WinePressPublishing
Great Books, Defined.

To order additional copies of this book call:
1-877-421-READ (7323)
or please visit our website at
www.WinePressbooks.com

If you enjoyed this quality custom-published book,
drop by our website for more books and information.

www.winepresspublishing.com
"Your partner in custom publishing."